MW01275688

From Sadness to Gladness

March 21/2018

To

Keith + Martha —

Thank you For your Friendship
and love —

God Bless you with peace,
Joy and happiness —

Teresa Ivy

From Sadness to Gladness

Terrence Morrissey

Copyright 2017 by Terrence Morrissey.
All rights reserved

ISBN: 1979017247
ISBN 13: 9781979017244

This book and/or any parts thereof, may not be reproduced in any form, stored in any
retrieval system, or transmitted in any form by any means including, but not limited to,
electronic, mechanical, photocopy, recording, or otherwise – without the prior written
permission of the author or his assigns. The contents including any and all pictures and/
or letters are legally copyrighted material and are the sole property of the author.

Introduction
By Jim McGregor

Creative people look at the world through a different lens than most. Some may see a foggy morning as just another obstacle on their drive to work while the creative eye will conjure ghosts and spirits moving through the mist and hear echoes that others will miss.

A writer will wake at three in the morning and scramble for their glasses and a pen and paper because just the right sentence or phrase has moved quickly and softly across the writing pad of their sleeping mind.

Perhaps sleep won't come because the right word or the perfect title is just there on the tip of their tongue or hiding in the deep folds of that imaginative brain.

The writer can sit in his office chair at his desk, a cup of coffee ready at his side, sharpened pencils ready and a clear computer screen in front of him, and not a word will come. He can pull and yank on his creativity but, like a stubborn mule in a warm stall, the words refuse to move.

But if the writer is driving past a field of waving wheat or a stand of October maples, with no pen and paper at hand, the words will tumble out like a cascading waterfall and he will struggle to find some way to contain them.

While pushing a grocery cart through a crowded store, the glimpse of a pretty girl or a young family will invoke memories and the words will start filling the grocery cart and spill on to the floor if he has no way to capture them.

The creative eye will see poetry in the rain and hear it in the rumble of thunder. The creative heart will feel poetry at the announcement of a new born or in the eulogy at a Celebration of Life.

The muse arrives at all hours of the day or night. It comes sneaking in on a scent or a tune. It slams in unexpectedly in the middle of a conversation or TV show. The writer learns not to wait for it, not to expect it, but to just accept it when it arrives.

When the creative person becomes so bold as to share their work with the world, to put their words into a book and display them for all to see, it is truly a leap of faith. Many of their poems are raw emotions or secret memories that are now out there for all to see.

The writer does not want you to put his work on a shelf and display it in pristine condition like a trophy. It is meant to be beside your easy chair or your night table, easily accessible for when you need comfort or inspiration.

He wants to see the corners of your favorites turned over so you can continuously find them easily and if there is a ring from a coffee cup on the cover that is even better for it shows his works have become part of your daily routine.

Consider this book to be good medicine for anything that ails you and prescribe yourself a healthy, daily dose

Dedication

I have been writing for a great many years, some five books self-published and many, many short stories and poems making their way into newspapers, magazines and such. I was master of ceremonies for a group stage act for fifteen years. My personal life due to an alcohol addiction has been one of turmoil and strife. Sure there were many moments of some sort of peace and joy but they were fleeting. The most difficult task I have ever undertaken is writing the dedication of this book...."From Sadness to Gladness."

I want to dedicate this book and the writings herein to the memory of my son Michael. Michael passed away on March 16, 2017 at the age of 51. Michael had a life of that was plagued with much sorrow due to a drug problem that he had. Michael had, on many occasions, worked hard at giving up the drugs and there were intervals where he was 'clean' for many, many months and a few times for a couple of years.

Michael worked hard to stay clean and he dedicated his life to helping others to do the same. Mike never gave up on anyone that sought him out for help. There was a period of about two years while Mike was working at a rehab centre where he was required, in order to help those in his care, to drive them to various meeting and different places. Unfortunately Mike had lost his driver's licence and he asked me to help him out. I was honored to be my son's driver for a little over two years. It was gratifying and gave my own life some deep purpose. One day I surprised Mike by going down to the courthouse and paying off all his fines, etc..His smile when he held his re-captured drivers Licence in his hand was a priceless moment.

I watched Michael as he interacted with those under his care. Mike was always gentle, kind and understood, without judgement, what those individuals were going through. I miss Mike; I miss him a lot, as I miss my other children that I was never there for due to my own addiction. An affliction that I was delivered from much too late in life, but grateful to be sober for almost 43 years as of this writing.

So to Mike, who also was a writer, I dedicate all that is within these pages. You can check out, on the index page, under "From Sadness to Gladness" to read what Mike was like and how his life ended. You can also check out one of the poems that he wrote titled "Untitled." Here you will find Michael, the son that I miss.

Terrence Morrissey

Appreciation

I want to express my gratitude and my sincere appreciation to my friend and fellow writer Jim McGregor for his very valuable assistance, understanding and patience as he previewed the work in this book. His obvious sympathetic understanding of me as a person and a writer will always be appreciated.

There were times while I was going through some of life's trials that Jim stood by with wisdom and understanding....for that enormous and sensitive part of his personality I will be forever grateful.

Jim writes for the Langley Times, here in Langley BC as a feature writer and his column, should you care to look it up, will at all times, entertain you and leave you with a feeling that you just read something very, very worthwhile. Also you will find three pieces of Jim's own writing in this book.

And I am indebted to John Attewell, another great friend. I appreciated John's friendship whenever he showed up for a cup of coffee and some much needed conversation. Always appreciating his suggestions.

OTHER BOOKS BY THE AUTHOR
Can be seen on Amazon.com or at your local bookstore

1. "ROBERT KENNEDY....THE FINAL DIVE" The author, Terrence Morrissey, was one of the last persons' to spend a vacation with the then Senator and presidential hopeful, Robert

F. Kennedy, vacationing in the Bahamas, just shortly prior to Mr. Kennedy's assassination. Terrence has recorded this once in a lifetime adventure with 'never before seen' pictures of Mr. Kennedy spear fishing, including personal letters. A spear fishing adventure well worth reading.

2. "DARK CORNERS" (Based on a true story)

A Christian commits a murder and is sentenced to sixteen years in a maximum security prison. He has to decide to be true to his faith or deny it in order to survive. No one has lived long who has walked around prison with a bible under his arm. A truly compelling story with all the sadness of violence, death hatred and love.

3. "WORDS OF LOVE" (Romantic Poetry)
4. "ABORTION, EUTHANASIA AND INFANTICIDE"
5. "A CHRISTIAN COUNSELOR'S GUIDEBOOK."

Terrence Morrissey
Email: terrence1@shaw.ca
Fax 604-534-2889

A Beautiful Expression Of Love

Sitting atop a hill one day I saw your smile amongst the clouds
Strolling along a garden pathway I felt the presence of your heartbeat
Beneath a golden moon on a star filled night I fell in love with you
once again
A rainbow, one early morn, announced the presence of your spirit
within me

Alone, as the evening fades, the memory of your perfume consumes
my senses
Memories of our first kiss caresses my heart as a teardrop comes
into view
A nightingale sings a mournful song of love and my spirit arises
out of self
A dancing star reminds me of the sparkle in your lovely eyes

You are so very beautiful I scarce can breathe as I see your face before me
A vision of your loveliness embraces my senses and
my heart beats louder
But all of this fades like the mist of the morning and my heart cries
"be still"
Then I hear the sound of your sweet voice as you whisper "I miss you."

Holding you close as we embrace in an embraceable love
Holding your soft and tender body close to mine
The love I see in your beautiful eyes
Tells me that you truly do miss me

And for that beautiful expression of love I am forever grateful

Terrence Morrissey

A Billowing Cloud

Favored tresses swaying gently in the wind
Her blushing face all aglow with laughter
The beauty of her eyes held my heart captive
As she shyly peeked from behind a golden moon

Never have I known her, only heard the music in her name
While a melancholy orchestra make a heavenly sound
And a choir of angels sang a perfumed song of love
To quiet the tempest of passion in her heart

A petal from a rose fell gently to the ground
As the sun once more kissed the smile upon her face
The morning mist, stirred about by a gentle breeze
Wrote the name of my beloved across life's meadow

And there she skipped across a rainbow
On a beautiful sunlit morn
After the stars of the night were gone
My beloved waltzed across a billowing cloud

Terrence Morrissey

A Butterfly Said It All

It was a sunny and peaceful morning
Before the birds began to sing
The sun crept over the horizon
And the flowers began to bloom

I awoke with a feeling of serenity
My soul at peace with the world
In a whisper I heard God call my name
Surprise and awe overtook me

I heard the voice of God declare
A sweet sound like the voice of an angel"
"My love is forever kind and unending
Be still and know that you belong to me"

Could God ever show me that gentleness?
I mused as I contemplated His words
Then in a picture beyond belief He showed me
A beautiful butterfly nestled amongst the flowers

There is a picture of God's love for you and the world
A picture of serenity, beauty and gentleness
More than man could ever imagine
Not a word more was needed for that butterfly said it all

Terrence Morrissey

A Castle In My Heart

There are kings that live in castles
There are knights that live there too
Sometimes one can find a prince
All waiting to show their love

There are millionaires all 'round the world
And billionaires do abound
Many handsome men who are also debonair
Would love to hold your hand in theirs

But the greatest love, the love of loves
A love that will last tenderly and forever
Is the love that I have for you, my treasured one
All held securely in a Castle in my heart

Terrence Morrissey

A City Full Of Churches

A city full of churches, great preachers and lettered men.
Grand music, choirs and organs, if all this fails what then?
Good workers, eager and earnest who labor hour by hour
But where oh where my brother is God's almighty power?

Refinement and education, they want the very best
Their plans and schemes are perfect, they give themselves no rest
They get the best of talent, they try their uttermost
But what they need, my brother, is God and the Holy Ghost.

We may spend time and money and preach from wisdom, love all
But education only, will keep God's children poor
God wants not worldly education, He seeks no smiles to win
But what is needed brother, is that we deal with sin.

It is the Holy Spirit that quickeneth the soul
God will not take man's worship, nor bow to man's control
No matter how innovative it may be, it is foolishness on the whole
So come now my friend and seek God to save your very soul

Author Unknown

A Flower And A Song

Sleepily, one morning, I saw a figure walking in my garden
She walked amongst a garden bouquet of flowers
Captivating were the flowers arrayed in a thousand colors
The figure, standing alone, was so much more beautiful

An enchanting fragrance slowly lifted to the sun
The figure, moving as in a dream, smiled an entrancing smile
A love song satisfied the morning quiet from a lone songbird
Alas the song of the shadowy figure was all the sweeter

The shadow, slightly turning, saw me gazing upon her beauty
Now smiling a smile of loveliness, cast over a disappearing shoulder
Vanished, as a song bird called, once again, among the flowers
In an instant my heart joined in a song of happiness

Terrence Morrissey
Copyright 2009

A Gentle Kiss

I SAW A RAIBOW IN THE SKY
I FELT A GENTLE BREEZE UPON MY LIPS
THE FEELING OF SOFTNESS THAT I FELT
WAS AS A BUTTERFLY SETTLING UPON A ROSE
AND I KNEW THAT YOUR LIPS HAD TOUCHED MINE

Terrence Morrissey

A Glance Across The Sea

Why dost thee glance across the sea?
Wishing thine lover home soon to be
Battles fought, some won, and some lost
A broken heart, a body torn, thus the cost

A thousand embraces down by the shore
Lovers united, families together once more
Alas, alone you stand just waiting for he
Lonely and sad as you glance across the sea

Terrence Morrissey

A Green Eyed Beauty And A Horse Called Durango

Her short blondish hair blows gently in the wind
As she sits in the saddle with her head held high
Her eyes, an emerald green, seemingly dance as she smiles
And the sun kisses her spirit aglow with the love of her horse

His name is Durango and his soul is held in her hands
Two together moving as one gliding along nature's pathway
His head upturned as he moves gallantly forward
Her smile exposing to the world a beauty so rare

Beautiful is her name and an adventurer she has always been
With two beautiful children gifted to her care by God
Her green eyes take on a sparkle whence she talks about them
A son, a daughter, and a horse named Durango three spirits to tame

With her hair blowing in the wind and green eyes all aglow
She makes her way through life sharing laughter and joy with all
Sadness upon a face so beautiful is at times there for all to see
Since the blues of life had been her companion for many a year

Dawn appeared one misty morning pushing aside the gloom of the night
Standing in a meadow against an early morning cloud was a horse
called Durango
Now, as one, with the wind at her back, rides a green eyed beauty,
eyes all aglow

A pretty green eyed beauty riding like the wind on a mighty horse called Durango

Terrence Morrissey

A Heart Just Like God

The sun kissed your cheek one early morn
As a gentle breeze caressed your sweet face
A blossom bloomed as you walked by
And a thousand bouquets burst upon the scene

My heart was jealous of all these things
Because they had that moment with you
But wait! I exclaimed one day
As I stood with rejoicing in my heart

God has sent the sun to kiss your cheek
He sent a gentle breeze to caress your sweet face
He made the blossom bloom as you walked by
All because you have a heart just like God

Terrence Morrissey

A Heart Of Pain

OH WHAT PAIN SUFFERS MY HEART
WHEN UPON THE EVENING WE ARE APART
ALTHOUGH MY HEART DOTH SEARCH IN VAIN
NOT A WORD OR SIGH DOTH EASE MY PAIN

WHEN ONCE I AWOKE UPON THE MORN
WITH ABANDONED HEART SAD AND FORLORN
WITH TEARFUL EYE AND BROKEN HEART
I LAMENT THE DAY THAT WE DID PART

ONE DAY YET OUR GOD WILL SPEAK
AND I WILL FEEL YOUR BREATH UPON MY CHEEK
AS TWILIGHT PEEKS BENEATH A SKY SO GRAND
WE WILL EMBRACE AS ONE AS GOD DID PLAN

Terrence Morrissey

A Love Poem For A Princess

Favored tresses swaying gently in the wind
Her blushing face all aglow with laughter
The beauty of her eyes held my heart captive
As she shyly peeked from behind a golden moon

My heart all aglow heard only the music in her name
While a melancholy orchestra made a heavenly sound
And a choir of angels sang a perfumed song of love
To quiet the tempest of passion in my heart

A petal from a rose fell gently to the ground
As the sun once more kissed the smile upon her face
The morning mist, stirred about by a gentle breeze
Wrote the name of my beloved across life's meadow

She skipped across a rainbow one sunlit morn
After the stars of the night were gone
She waltzed across the silver lining of my heart
And my sweet princess held my heart captive for eternity

Terrence Morrissey

A Memory Made In Heaven

I COULD HEAR HER SOFTLY BREATHING
AS MY BELOVED
SLEPT GENTLY IN MY ARMS

Terrence Morrissey

A New Life Thus Begun

Gently kissing her lips I saw her smile
As a candle glowed with flickering flame
And angels danced upon a moonbeam

Daybreak caressed her where she lay
As a golden sun disturbed the morning mist
She smiled as she gently nestled in my arms
The promise of a new life thus begun

Terrence Morrissey

A Pretty Girl A Cup Of Coffee And A Puppy

It was early in the morning when the sun began to shine
And the flowers in the fields began their early morning bloom
Songbirds began to sing an early morning song of love
But nothing prepared me for the beauty I was about to see

She stood there all alone a picture of loveliness no one could deny
A cup of coffee in one hand and a puppy by her side
The smile upon her face revealed the beauty that was inside
Sweet and gentle tresses caressed her lovely face

She looked at me with charming curiosity in her smile
"Good Morning" spoke she with a voice delightful and captivating
As the sun kissed her lovely face and a song bird sang a song of love
Day dawned to a rare and beautiful sight, a pretty girl a cup of coffee
and a puppy

Terrence Morrissey

A Rose Without A Kiss

The moment I saw you walk across that floor
A rose was planted in my heart
You watered that rose every time we kissed
And the rose began to bloom

Watered every day and sometimes twice a day
Becoming a rosebush with blossoms on every branch
The rosebush leaves turned a brilliant green
And held each rose in a tender embrace

Now alas without a kiss no water did appear
The rosebush withered and started to die
And the roses did lose their luster
As a tear drop fell from my heart

Without a kiss to keep those roses in bloom
My heart did lose its luster too
And each day I long for a kiss
So that the rose in my heart will bloom again

A tear drop fell from out of my heart
But could not bring those flowers to bloom
Sadly the rose that lived within my heart
Became a rose without a kiss

Terrence Morrissey

A Shattered Dream

I held her close, oh so very close
Her head resting gently upon my breast
Her naked body moving closer, ever closer
A trembling lingering kiss as her lips sought mine

A sigh so deep held breathless for eternity or so it seemed
Stirring with emotion, a tender caress touching even my very soul
"Hold me closer" she whispered as our emotions stirred
I scarce could breathe as I turned to embrace her once more

Our bodies now as one, tender, touching cleaving in a deep embrace
Reaching in the twilight of a golden moonbeam
As it shone its golden light upon her sweet tresses
We once again loved as lovers who never before had loved

I held her close, fearful that my dream would end
As the fragrance of her love and beauty
Sent my senses reeling and my heart to pounding
My sweetheart now owns my heart and soul for eternity

Alas, it was all but a dream, and I awoke with a start
My sweet lover, never again will I feel her embrace
Whilst her heart was alive but for a short time
A golden moon still stirs my heart to love, but never again

My heart is broken; I am left with but a shattered dream

Terrence Morrissey

A Simple Thing

Why shed a teardrop over such a simple thing?
I ask myself as I lay there by your side.
Reaching out I touched you and you turned to face me,
Our lips met and the teardrops on my cheek mingled with yours.

In an instant I knew from whence came the teardrop,
It came from the depth of my very being.
Holding back nothing I let the teardrops flow,
Shame overtook me, men aren't supposed to cry.

Reaching out once again, I touched your soft, sweet self,
As before our lips met, one again your tears mingled with mine.
The gentleness of your kiss told me that my tears were not in vain,
For you knew and understood why my pain was so great.

Never have I loved so completely or with such abandon,
Out of the deep recesses of your heart I heard a song,
There in the darkness your song became my song,
Two hearts beat as one and the pain in my heart exploded.

When I told you that I loved you completely,
You whispered softly, 'I know you do,' and I was fulfilled.
Thank you my beloved for giving yourself to me
And letting me give myself to you.

By Terrence Morrissey

A Sleep Over Once Again

It all started so innocently, a conversation was all it was to be
Looking into those beautiful big brown
eyes my heart sang a different song
She drew herself closer to me and smiled a beguiling smile
At first it was just a kiss, a simple beautiful kiss, it took me by surprise

As she took my hand in hers I could feel the warmth of her finger tips
Just a little squeeze was all it was meant to be, or so I thought
But her fingers played a sweet melody up and down my arm
Quivering, tingling hot shots ran up and down my spine

I silently told my quick beating heart to be still
as it thundered in my ears
But still my heart would not be and the uproar rumbled on deep
within my breast
Reaching out I took her and held her close to my beating heart
Kissing her sweet lips I knew the conversation was over

Silently together we walked down the long and soft carpeted hallway
She sighed a sigh of love as we headed for the bedroom and the dream
that lay within
The candles were lit and the bedsheets white
as she nestled in my arms
It was early in the morning when my beloved, snuggled in my arms,
softly whispered
That was quite a sleepover, let's do it once again

Terrence Morrissey

A Song Of Love

I FELT HER HEART BEAT GENTLY AGAINST MY CHEST
AS I HELD THE SOFTNESS OF HER BODY IN MY ARMS
THE LOVELINESS WITHIN HER, HELD MY HEART CAPTIVE
A SLAVE TO LOVE AS A LEAF DRIFTED
SLOWLY TO THE GROUND

THE WHISPER OF THE WIND CARESSED THE SMILE UPON
HER FACE
THE TOUCH OF A GOLDEN MOONBEAM SHONE
BEAUTIFULLY IN HER EYES
A STAR TWINKLING BRIGHTLY SPOKE OF
JOYFUL DAYS TO COME
AND A NIGHTINGALE SANG A SONG OF LOVE

Terrence Morrissey

A Songbird And A Faded Tear Drop

One night as I walked alone under the light of a lonely star
My mind did wonder about days long gone by and oh so far away
A careless breeze, a falling leaf, a songbird singing a lonesome song
Memories did capture all these things, but alas my broken heart did weep

When once we walked, hand in hand, beneath that same lonely star
But so many years have gone by that only a weeping heart remains
A full moon shining in a clear night sky as your lips touched mine
Your smile spoke a thousand words and promised
a lifetime of happy bliss

A night owl caroled a forlorn ballad as you kissed me with a sleepy smile
An ample moon spun a web much like a golden
veil across that precious kiss
I heard you whisper "I love you" as a nightingale sang
a promise of love forever
The moon and the songbird linger on as a teardrop
caresses my broken heart

I walk, once more, by the light of a lonely star and the caress
of a careless breeze
I hear that same songbird singing his lonesome song and
I sigh a lonesome sigh
Memories are all that remain of a shining golden moon
and a sweet and lingering kiss
Turning, I walk away as the song of the songbird fades and
I wipe a tear from my eye

Terrence Morrissey

A Teasing Kiss

I saw her standing in the noonday sun
As a gentle breeze kissed her wine colored lips
Her cheeks aglow were also gently caressed
And the breeze tenderly shifted her golden locks

Captured in a moment of time my heart did yield
Love sprung forth as a surging tide held in endless wonder
Seized by a beauty so unique that my heart stood in silent awe
What now, cried the spirit of love within me, what now?

The noonday sun turned to a crimson sunset
As we strolled, hand in hand by a lake of blue
A golden moon smiled at a beauty so rare indeed
Hearts entrapped and held captive for time without end

A teasing bewitching kiss as a night bird sang
A caressing glance into her dancing eyes
My heart reaching to embrace her heart
Encountered her smile and my fate was sealed

Terrence Morrissey

A Wedding Vow
(My Promise to You)

This is my promise to you, my beloved
That as long as you allow me
I will cherish you and honour you
In all of the things I say and do

My promise is as faithful as the sunrise
As long lasting as the skies above
It shines more brilliant than the brightest star
Never to falter whether I am near or far

For my darling if I promise in the words of man
My pledge is as weak as the weakest child
But my word is shrouded in the love of an honourable man
You can count on it always to be valiant and true

What good would I be if I could move a mountain?
Or swim the largest ocean, or be the slayer of dragons
Or bear the whole world upon my shoulders for all to see
And yet fail you and render my promise barren

No, my beloved I will love you with patience
I will boast of God's gift to me, which is you
I will not seek my own fulfilment but yours first, always
In troubled times I will persevere and our God will see me through

You have made my life favoured, even more precious that breath itself
Your kindness and tenderness have won me utterly, forever
If you wear this ring that comes with a promise of my undying love
I now do commit to you my life, completely and forever

When the trials of life and love overtake us
And around us the waters are disquieted
Invading even our very souls
I will fall to my knees and call upon our God

And He will deliver us into calmness and peace
For His promise is the greatest promise of all
That never will our God forsake us or leave us
His love is the strength that I will call upon
To keep my promise to you, my beloved

By Terrence Morrissey

A Woman Like You

I may not always show it
But it's a feeling deep inside
How very blessed I am
To have a woman like you

When I think of all you mean to me
The happiness you've brought to my heart
All because of the sweetness of yourself
And the surrender of your heart and soul

The confidence you have placed in me
To protect the security of your heart
Has given me the ability to love you deeper still
And to tell you how important your love is to me

Thank you for loving me the way you do
And thank you for allowing me to love you also
When you say "I love you" with such pureness of your heart
Then I know how blessed I am to be loved by a woman like you

Terrence Morrissey

Adorable

Dawn broke and songbirds all together sang a song of love
Flowers bloomed and opened their petals to a new day
A blue and brilliant sky spoke of peace and calmness
A lake's clear waters rushing on by whistled that love was in the air

Heaven's doors opened and silver lined clouds
poured out love upon the earth
A golden sun captured the hearts of early morning lovers
out for a stroll
A rainbow with uncountable colors spoke of the joys yet to come
And an early morning breeze caressed the smiles of
beauty everywhere

But nothing, not the moon, the stars, a rainbow or songbirds
Nor the flowers that bloomed in the early morning dawn
Not even the trill of a lone songbird could capture the loveliness
Of the adorable one whose beauty has captured my heart forever

Terrence Morrissey

Adoring You

How do I adore you, you might ask
And I, scarcely breathing, would answer
Let me kiss you with the kisses of my mouth
For your kiss is more delightful than a morning's sunrise

Your cheeks, aflame with the color of passion, are as velvet to touch
The fragrance of your perfume sets my soul and body aflame
How breathtaking are your eyes, careless and seductive
How wonderful you are, a delicate and beautiful flower

When at twilight I hold you in my arms
I drink of your sweetness as at a banquet
I am aroused by your very being,
Our eyes meet and love is held for eternity

Your smile captivates me and beckons me closer
I reach out and in a twinkling we are one
You fade into my very existence, our lips touch
Our bodies, inseparable, are as one

All night long upon our bed, we speak of beautiful days to come
Of future torrid nights and dreams yet to redeem
Once more you rise up to meet me and our bodies are as one
Gently you sigh that you love me and I whisper that I adore you
And in an instant we are paradise bound

By Terrence Morrissey

All Over Again

My precious beloved
Today I fell in love with you all over again
I loved you the first moment our eyes met
And I loved you more the first time our lips touched
How blessed I am to have you in my life
And how blessed I am to call you 'My Beloved'
Thank you for loving me
For tomorrow I will fall in love with you
All over again

Terrence Morrissey

An Amazing Gal

You are such an amazing gal
You are one of a kind
Sensitive, lovely and sparkling
A heart molded personally by God

Filled with tenderness, and kindness
A heart searching to give love
A soul and mind trimmed in gold
A spirit that searches for the lonely

The inner you holding your loved one near
Comforting those whose spirit has been damaged
A light shining in the darkness of another's pain
My beloved, God smiles when he sees your radiance

Your love of life and of others
Casts a glowing love 'round about
And touches the very heart and soul
Of all who are near to you,
Thank you for making my heart so happy.

Terrence Morrissey

An Angel In My Arms

Last night as I lay down by your side
My heart was filled with a happy anticipation
From the warmth of your body so close to mine
A whispered sigh as you moved so very close

The night stars shone as brilliant lights in a cloudless sky
And a moonbeam paved a golden road into my heart
A nightingale sang a song of love and I felt the beat
of your loving heart
As you nestled your sweet self into my waiting arms

The night was sweet and the loving sweeter still
Your lips sought out mine and we became as one
A smile and honeyed embrace as two lovers held close
I awoke to a morning songbird with an angel in my arms

Terrence Morrissey

An Irishman's Dream

Romantic he was, romantic he is and romantic he will always be
He dreamt dreams always hoping his dream would come true some day
He has always been a lover and a lover he will always be
But his one true love has alluded him and left and
empty spot in his heart

Search he might and search he did, never doubting that one day he
would meet her
One day he glanced across a crowded room and there his lover stood
His heart almost stopped, without taking his eyes from her beauty
he stood before her
She looked at him and then he knew that from that moment
they would never be apart

Her brown eyes sparkled and her smile enchanting as her
voice as velvet spoke
"Hello" she said with a twinkle of understanding in her
eyes for she knew all
The Irishman smiled and took her hand in his as he looked
deep into her eyes
The pact was sealed with only one word being spoken and
the 'Hello' said it all

They walked out under a silvery moon with her hand held lovingly in his
Under the branches of a large old tree a breeze caressed her parted lips
His lips touched hers and she responded with a kiss so full of love
And every night the lovers stand hand in hand as she touches
her lips to his

Terrence Morrissey

An Ode To An Old Man With A Broken Heart

A lonely old man stood before the pearly gates
His face was withered, scarred and old
He stood before his God to be admitted to the fold
He knew his chances were slim as he remembered years gone by

The years flashed by and in the remembering his pain was great
Ignoring his role as husband and father he heeded the call of another
There was no pain at the time it happened,
his senses were dulled with lust
Walking away and leaving them there he felt no pang of guilt at all

What have you done, the Lord did ask, to gain admittance here
Your terrible actions of yesteryear have seared even
my heart with pain
I know Sir, the man replied, there was something wrong with me
And it wasn't until many years later that I realized what I had done

I have suffered lo these many years with a pain that
no one can explain
Every day when I awoke I cried myself to sleep again
I could not face another day and suicide was my constant companion
But cowardice always raised its ugly head and no guts had
I do the deed

There was not a moment that I did not think of the family
I left behind

Mother toiling day and night to feed and comfort the children
and ease their terrible pain
I still see her there, though many years have passed,
with a smile upon her face
As she worked to raise those lovely children,
a job I had promised to do

My pain grew greater at what I had done with tears
shed sometimes on the hour
I wanted to kill myself for what I had done, but cowardice
kept me from the deed
My punishment is great and it is all I deserve and maybe even more
For this past half a century I have been in agony,
never a moment of peace

Sir please take me to your heart and don't forsake me
as I forsook my family
Please Let me past these golden gates and let me find some peace
Forgiveness is what I desire although I am sure I am not worthy
But, dear God I cannot face another day of pain and
I cannot shed another tear.

The pearly gates swung open, Jesus stood there with a smile,
happiness on His face
Come in, Jesus spoke, with a heart so full of joy,
we've been waiting for you
Your broken heart speaks loudly of repentance and I was
happy to pay the price
So that you and others just like you can spend eternity
in this here paradise

Terrence Morrissey

As Long As You Walk Back In

The words really stung and were hurtful to the core
But I deserved them and that hurt even more
Guarding my temper and thinking first, how hard was that to do

Walking across the room and grabbing my jacket
I headed for the door
Who needs this, I thought out loud, I deserve better treat-
ment or so I thought
She watched me go, with a frown and bewilderment
showing on her face
Perplexed she muttered "What could I have done"
as I headed for that door

"Well it was all quite clear, I shot back, don't you realize?"
When you said "Come sit beside me" and let's cuddle close"
I moved from my seat with a great big grin right across my face
I spoke out loud, "Now this is what I am here for"
and started to her side

"Where are you going?" Said she, moving the little blan-
ket closer to her side
"Why I am accepting your warm and suggestive invitation" I replied
"No, she jumped half out of her seat, I wasn't talking to you."
Reaching across and patting the blanket she said "Come here Nicky."

I almost fainted and stopped dead in my tracks,
Nicky was her little poodle
"Are you serious?" I asked in a weak and defeated voice
as I stared at that dog

"Of course I am, we always watch TV together"
and the dog was by her side
I grabbed for my jacket and opened that great big door and
down the stairs I went

It only took me thirty minutes to realize the foolishness of my error
Picking up the telephone, I apologized and ask to be forgiven
"I belong to you and you belong to me" said that forgiving voice
"You can walk out anytime as long as you walk back in."

Terrence Morrissey
(Based on an actual experience)

Beautiful

Dawn broke and songbirds all together sang a song of love
Flowers bloomed and opened their petals to a new day
A blue and brilliant sky spoke of peace and calmness
A lake's clear waters rushing on by whistled that love was in the air

Heaven's doors opened and silver lined clouds poured out love
upon the earth
A golden sun captured the hearts of early morning lovers out
for a stroll
A rainbow with uncountable colors spoke of the joys yet to come
And an early morning breeze caressed the smiles
of beauty everywhere

But nothing, not the moon, the stars, a rainbow or songbirds
Nor the flowers that bloomed in the early morning dawn
Not even the trill of a lone songbird could capture the loveliness
Of one so beautiful whose loveliness has captured my heart forever

Terrence Morrissey

Beautiful And Charming is my Sweet Love

What secrets lay behind those eyes?
What depth of happiness or loneliness?
Oh well, thought the world, never, ever will we know
Until that fateful day when first they saw her

A graceful movement, as beneath a misty moon
Did catch their attention for one breathless moment
With poise stood a woman as lovely as one could be
Attractively delightful hair outlined a graceful face

Her demeanor was lovely, quiet and serene
As she stood there quietly observing all that occurred
But wait, what sadness on her sweet face did appear
Was it a look of delightful curiosity, or possibly more?

How absolutely beautiful, the world did exclaim
For never had their eyes beheld a beauty so unexpected
Not even, when long ago, they glanced upon Mona Lisa's smile
Silently, the heart sang a song of sweet delight to see one so beautiful

Mona Lisa's smile captured the hearts of men as under a spell
But on this day, as a golden sunbeam touched the lips of one so lovely
All of heaven rejoiced and angels sang a song of thanks to God
For creating one as beautiful and charming and
lovely as my sweet love

Terrence Morrissey

Beauty Splendor and Love

There was beauty splendor and love everywhere
The birds sang a song to their Creator on high
Flowers turned their petals to their creator above
A rainbow appeared and brilliant colors did abound

The radiance of the sun winked at the whole of creation

But alas a teardrop fell upon the cheek of God
As He observed and thought about it all
There was pain and suffering and sadness did prevail
No birds sang, flowers never bloomed, the rainbow lost its color

All at once a Son did smile a smile upon the earth
At that moment swaying trees waved to the heavens
The birds sang a song of love, and a flower bloomed
A rainbow of brilliant colors looked down upon the earth

Up in the sky sparkling Golden gates swung open
There He stood and with one wave of His hand
The hand with the drops of blood where once it was pierced
The world, yet again, rejoiced in beauty, splendor and love

Terrence Morrissey

Captured

Dawn broke and songbirds all together sang a song of love
Flowers bloomed and opened their petals to a new day
A blue and brilliant sky spoke of peace and calmness
A lake's clear waters rushing on by whistled that love was in the air

Heaven's doors opened and silver lined clouds poured out love
upon the earth
A golden sun captured the hearts of early morning lovers out
for a stroll
A rainbow with uncountable colors spoke of the joys yet to come
And an early morning breeze caressed the smiles of
beauty everywhere

But nothing, not the moon, the stars, a rainbow or songbirds
Nor the flowers that bloomed in the early morning dawn
Not even the trill of a lone songbird could capture the loveliness
Of the one I love whose beauty has captured my heart forever

Terrence Morrissey

Climb Higher

9/11

A Tribute to the New York City Firefighters

"Keep on Climbing", says the Captain,
"Up through the smoke and smell";
"Keep on climbing", says the Captain,
"I think I heard somebody yell!"
"Keep on climbing", says the Captain
"Alive or dead, Not ours to tell."
"Keep on climbing", calls the Captain
"Forget about your pain!"
"Keep on climbing", shouts the Captain,
"We have a few more floors to gain"
"Keep on climbing", yells the Captain
"We will bring them down again!"
"Keep on climbing", cries the Captain
"If I can so can you!"
"Keep on climbing", orders the Captain
"Right now I need your best from you!"
"Keep on climbing", screams the Captain,
"Forget about those sounds!"
"It's just some girders twisting
And some concrete falling down";
"Keep on climbing", whispers the Captain;
"Climb right up to that light!"
"Right up to that sunshine,
"No smoke to smell,
"No fire to fight!"
"Keep on climbing", sings the Captain,
"That Angel's hand will lead the way!"

"Rest boys", sighs the Captain
"You did your job, today!"
"Keep on climbing", prays Our Captain:
"Eyes raised, headed for the top."
"And when you're tired
And feel like quitting,
Remember them,
They didn't stop!"

By Jim McGregor
Langley City Fire Chief
Langley, B.C. Canada

Dancing In Heaven

She danced as one dancing on a cloud
A rainbow gently hugged her round about
She smiled a smile and the birds burst into song
The first rose of summer never looked so enchanting

My heart stopped, or so it seemed, for a second or two
My gaze I could not draw away from her loveliness
As she danced her eyes caught my gaze and I turned aside
The blue in her eyes was as the blue of an early morning sky

Be still, I cried as my heart did flutter, be still and weep not
For the one before you stands as an angel before the Lord
She speaks of you in heavenly places just as one in love
The angels consented and she now abides deep within my heart

Turning once more I watched as she danced across the heavens
A bewitching smile of love adorns her face and she laughs
Dancing into my arms I stood transfixed as she took me by the hand
And now we dance together, forever…. our hearts beat as one

Terrence Morrissey

Dancing In My Mind

A candle flickered in the darkened room
As shadows danced crazily across the wall
Pictures of yesteryear paraded through my mind
Keeping time with the dancing figures on the wall

Sweat caressed my aching head and fell amid my tears
The dancing shadows kept time with my aching heart
Light and shadows deprived my pining mind of rest
Tossing, turning and longing pained my soulful heart

All the yesterdays silently becoming in the night as one
The shadows on the wall now dancing with my memories
Sleep evades me once again as I am reminded of errors past
The candle is no more and the dancing within my mind ceases

Terrence Morrissey

Dawn

Dawn has broken with a bright shimmering glow
And your smile captivates me in that golden flow
I see within the deep recess of your eyes
A sparkle and warmth that holds no goodbyes

Your breasts rise with each breath you take
And all for wanting you my body does ache
I touch the softness beneath the sheets
Your racing heart thus counts the beats

The light of the moon caresses your body
You reach out to me and your smile is naughty
Moving closer we once again embrace
As you move my mind to a heavenly place

Never more to wake alone
With only hope upon your mind
Now in your arms the happiness you hoped to find
Trust me my beloved, and fear not a night alone
I am here and now make you my own

Terrence Morrissey

Deep Is My Pain

My heart is light....my spirit soars and my happiness knows no bounds......on the outside.....but on the inside.....well that is another matter altogether....

Once, I fell in love....now, as time takes its toll, I find that I never fell out of love with that girl. Sometimes my love for her wells up so painfully in my heart that I wish I was dead....To avoid the pain that memories bring and knowing that I will never see her again and never hold her close to me once more, I penned these feelings...so that you too may know how deep is my pain.

I see her face in every sunrise and sunset....
I feel the warmth of her body next to mine,
Whenever the sun shines high in the heavens
It sends warmth throughout my body, soul and spirit.

Sometimes in the still of the night, as I lay upon my bed,
I can hear her softly breathing although I sleep alone.
In that moment my heart knows true and perfect happiness
It is the most glorious feeling that I could ever experience....

The next moment the pain is so all encompassing
That it makes one want to disappear altogether to erase
the hurt forever
To quiet the pain that sears my heart, mind, body and soul.
Oh, how absolutely painful it is to be in love...

From this day forward, I know I will never see
A sunrise as beautiful as the love I saw in your eyes
when first we did meet

Nor will I ever see a sunset as calm and as sweet as
when I first saw you sleeping
No, never will I see an enchanted forest as lovely as you
when I first saw you smile

No, no, not ever will my eyes behold an angel as divine nor as
sweet as you.
All these things I will never, ever see again in this lifetime.
No one has ever known the depth of agony that has touched my soul
Or how exceedingly deep is my pain.

Terrence Morrissey

Disco Dave And His Dancing Feet

He said he could dance and that was no lie
And all the girls agreed as they all sat by
Waiting their turn for a spin and a whirl
Each one hoping that they would be that girl

Disco Dave was the man they dreamed of
To take them to the dance floor and fulfill their dream
To be in his arms and to be held so close as they danced
They waited and prayed and some even cried

Here he comes, one was heard to shout
And then the door opened and Disco Dave came out
They crowded around him and took him by the arm
It was all accomplished due to Disco Dave's charm

Disco's arm was around her waist and the other held her hand in his
They started to move and to swing and sway
The crowd stood watching they had nothing to say then
one little gal spoke
With a voice so sweet, "Disco Dave has swept me off my feet"

After the dance was over, they left arm in arm
Off to Disco Dave's place as he spoke with plenty of charm

The sun rose early the very next day
I will never leave Disco Dave she was heard to say

His dancing is superb and warm to touch
But nothing can compare with his loving and such
Sleeping gently in his arms made her world complete
She fell in love with Disco Dave and his dancing feet

Terrence Morrissey

Don't Wait Another Day

She was young and beautiful
But no one ever brought her flowers
She fell in love one day
And flowers were on her mind

One day we married so young and in a hurry
But alas, I never brought her flowers
She always had flowers upon her mind
And saw them within her heart

The years came and the years flew by
And it seems I was always too busy
To think about those flowers
Someday, I said to myself, flowers she shall have

The children grew and had children of their own
I swore I would bring her flowers one day
But it seems there was always something else
I will bring her a bouquet I promised deep within my heart

Her hair turned to grey, her beauty always with her
And each day she thought of that beautiful bouquet
Tomorrow I will I said with a heart so full of love
But there was always something else that stole the time away

I bought her a single but beautiful rose today
I never should have waited to bring her that bouquet

Because today I knelt with a broken heart
And placed a single rose upon her grave

Terrence Morrissey

Eve And Her Partner Adam

Eve was not taken out of Adam's head to top him, neither out of his feet to be trampled on by him, but out of his side to be equal with him, under his arm to be protected by him, and near his heart to be loved by hi

Author Unknown

Eyes So Beautiful

The first fall of snow as it made white the meadows
The first fall leaf as it drifted slowly to the ground
The first summer butterfly as it alighted atop a spring flower
The first gentle rain of summer as it caressed the valleys
The first springtime trill of a mocking bird as it greeted a new day
The first time my heart was held captive for all eternity

When I think on all of these beautiful and wondrous things
I think of all of God's creation and I dream a dream
That my heart was captured forever and forever
The first time I saw all the wondrous beauty of God's creation
Was the moment I first looked into your eyes so beautiful

Terrence Morrissey

Five Little Words
"I'm So Proud Of You"

I'm so proud of you" I heard the woman say
She spoke into the telephone; a smile was in her voice
Then she also spoke these words, "and I love you"
Words can heal or hurt I once heard someone tell

So as she turned to face me, her smile said it all
The other person on the phone must have made her very happy
As I walked away I pondered the words that I heard that lady speak
Often we forget that words can build up or tear down

Proud with her head held high a halo almost there
She walked over to the counter and faced another customer
How can I help you, she spoke with words so sincere
And that smile and halo never left her or so it seemed to me

Of course beauty is in the eyes of the beholder, as the saying goes
And also in the words we hear, and I looked at her once more
I walked over to tell her how much the words she spoke meant to me
As I was in need of someone to say how proud they were of me

You are absolutely a blessing to me I spoke in a voice very low
As you were to your son or daughter on the other end of the line
That wasn't my son or daughter she exclaimed, it was my husband
How absolutely in love they must be and what joy she brought to him

Today, tell someone that you are very proud of them.

Terrence Morrissey

Flowers Gentle Beneath Our Feet

What has happened to my beloved?
In the morn you were no more
What has happened to my beloved?
I asked with a sigh and a broken heart

It is all so new and all so very strange
When once I glanced you were always there
Always you were part of me,
Lo these many, many years

What has happened to my beloved?
Is written in pain across my heart
In the early morning you were no more
And in the twilight as in the early morn

What has happened to my beloved?
Perplexing as it may seem
I know you are no more upon this earth
Yet you dwell daily within my heart

Alas, I no more ask, what has happened to my beloved
For my heart now knows peace and calmness
You have gone ahead as you always have
To prepare a place for our love to bloom, forever

One day, my beloved, in God's perfect time
I will walk again with you, your hand in mine

Eternally strolling across meadows so grand
With the fragrance of flowers gentle beneath our feet

Terrence Morrissey

For All Eternity

Just a gentle kiss on a moonlit night
Whence met our lips and I heard an Angel sing
And my love for you was sealed

God placed this love in my heart for you, my beloved
There it has stayed since the day you took my hand in yours
And there it will stay for all eternity

Terrence Morrissey

Forever Alone I Stand

Thunder rocked a cloudy sky
As lightening lit the morning
A lone bird huddled in fear
A forlorn cry of a startled wolf

Fear seizing a lonely heart
A tear drop falling upon the ground
A wasted smile startling a withered face
A sigh of pain emanating from within

Not another day, whispered a wretched voice
Pain and fear, and heartache I cannot face
My resolve is lost for I am abandoned
My beloved left as thunder rocked a cloudy sky

Once we smiled as we embraced, sharing a tender kiss
Holding hands as we strolled across meadows green
Lovers lost in the beating heart of one another
My beloved loves another, thus forever alone I stand

Terrence Morrissey

Forever Lovely

She all at once appeared out of the moonlight
As it sliced a golden path across the still water
Her beauty was enchanting, her smile captivating
I stood as one bewitched held and stilled

The golden shaft became a roadway of gold
As it made its way across the calmness of the sea
I stood beguiled as she strolled in an angel like walk
Across the pathway that the moon had created

Her footsteps were silent, her movement graceful
Closer she came as the gold of the moon danced in her eyes
I watched as the evening mist clung gently to her body
Revealing an angelic shape that defied the gods of the night

Silently she glided into my arms with a promise of love
Embracing, we danced beneath a moon so bright
It dazzled even the birds who sang a nightly song of love
She stands more beautiful than any and is forever lovely

Terrence Morrissey

From Sadness To Gladness
How God Turned A Father's
Broken Heart

From: DAD
Sent: Sunday, March 12, 2017 9:35:43 AM
To: Michael
Subject: Howdy

'morning Mike....just a short note to say "Howdy" and hope that all is well with you....hope things are looking up for you.....keep on trying Mike...please don't give up....the future may not look to good right now but if you keep on trying, praying and seeing, in your mind, the work that God can accomplish with you and your God given talents you will be delighted.
God bless you son,
Dad

From: "Michael
To: Dad
Sent: Tuesday, March 14, 2017 6:10:41 AM
Subject: Re: Howdy
Hi Dad. I'm ok still alive. In n out of hosp last couple weeks but finally feeling a tad bit better... haven't done anything bad for like 3 or 4 days now ..maybe 5. Not sure anymore just been sleeping lots... I hit my knees last night .so to speak...I was in bed already ... but I offered my life up to GOD & JESUS Again. I asked for forgiveness. And asked GOD to use me as he saw fit. This is something I haven't been able to do in years... as broken and lost as I am I just laid it down. I accepted

that I messed up all the incredible blessings he bestowed unto me and I know I turned on him and traded it all for feeling of the flesh to be with that woman... I feel like a complete fool. But hey... I made my bed after God blessed me with so many miracles... I chose to do it my way and WHAM here I am...back to broken starting from less than ZERO. Sick alone broke lost...all the things he saved me from before... so please pray for me that he hears my prayer...and can use my story to reach and maybe save others the same fate. It's a pain filled place to be...
Michael

From: "Dad"
To: "Michael
Sent: Tuesday, March 14, 2017 7:12:25 AM
Subject: Re: Howdy

Mike...my son, you just made your dad the happiest father in the world... how proud I am of you....I know that there is something inside of you that is bigger, better and more wonderful than even you or I realize... keep up the good work and just watch how God will use you in HIS determination to save and help others with your help. I have been and will always be praying for you. Please keep in touch and I will write again later...just woke up...going to have a coffee....
God bless you Michael,
Dad

On Saturday March 18 I received a telephone call from Michael's wife, informing me that Michael had passed away on the previous Thursday, March 16. Mike's heart failed and coupling that with his drug use it was too much for him. My own heart was broken in a million pieces. Michael and I had shared many, many wonderful moments together and have had email contact for many years. Mike always expressed, in those emails, how things were going with his life and it was not good. I did my best to encourage him always reminding him to look to God for the answers to his problems. Not ever preaching to him but just encouraging conversations. Looking back at Mike's email of March 14th and his determination to beat his drug habit and his recommitment to Jesus, his Saviour and to God and Mike's determination that if his life could just help one person he, Michael, would be happy.

God heard Michael's prayer and on Thursday, two days after his commitment and promise, God gave Michael the most wonderful gift of all. A place where there is no more suffering, no more pain and no more tears.

I was thinking of Michael on Thursday and the bible story about the prodigal son came to mind.... I saw Michael being welcomed into heaven as his Father God ran out to meet him...it made my heart very happy to see God give Michael a hug and say, with a loving voice....."Welcome home son."

I thank God for His love of Michael and also His love of countless others that He, God, has taken home to be with Himself, on streets paved with gold, where there is no more suffering, no more pain. Where eternal happiness is the fulfillment of God's promise.

I am happy to say..."Thanks God"....for turning my sadness into gladness....all because you truly did care about Michael. Michael also got his wish that if he could help just one person he, Michael, would be happy. Well, since this was written I am happy to report that more than "One" life has been helped and some lives have been changed forever.
Terrence Morrissey
A proud father of a wonderful son.

From Whence Did This Love Spring

Was it the way you took my hand
And held it with love in yours?

Was it the way you looked at me
With your beautiful and loving eyes?

Was it the way you cuddled up close and secure?
As we sat beneath a tree on a moonlit night?

Was it the when you touched your cheek to mine
As I held you in my arms and we waltzed as the music played?

Was it the thrill, joy and happiness that my heart felt
When you laughed and angels danced in your eyes?

Was it watching you look over your shoulder down by the lake
When, with a trembling heart, I handed you my life?

Was it the pride I felt as you shared share your happiness with me
When you boldly proclaimed your love for me?

No, my beloved, it was none of these that sealed my love for you

It was a gentle kiss on a moonlit night
Whence met our lips and I heard a thousand Angels sing

God placed the love in my heart for you, my beloved
And there it stays for all eternity

By Terrence Morrissey

Gravity....It Never Fails

Plant a seed of happiness and reap a harvest of joy. It's not really all about money. God has many fields just waiting for a seed to be sown. Sow seeds of friendship and get a harvest of friends. Plant a seed of a smile and reap a bountiful harvest of smiles. Sow seeds of kindness and you will reap a bountiful harvest of kindness at the exact time you need it most. Think about your own future harvest and how you want to be treated.... always remembering.... the seeds you are planting today will be your absolute harvest of tomorrow....God's promise of sowing and reaping is exactly like gravity.... it never fails.

Terrence Morrissey

Hand In Hand

It has been well said and many times over
That God holds the whole world in His hands
I even sang that song not so many years ago
Until one day on a sparkling sunlit morn

How is that possible, I exclaimed to the sky above
As I walked out under a rainbow smiling overhead
The happiness on my face a story it did tell
I could prove that saying was not right and here is how I know

How could it be possible for God to hold the whole world
in His hands?
When all one has to do is see the happiness in my heart and the smile
upon my face
The truth be told, the evidence is in and now you will understand
God holds the whole world in just one hand for His
other hand holds mine

Terrence Morrissey

Her Prayer

She bowed her head and closed her eyes and sighed a deep sigh
I listened as she talked to God about this and that in a low voice
Her voice was soft and sweet and a little more than determined
I had a funny feeling that she really had God's attention

She stopped for a minute after chatting with God
about her children
Then she continued, holding God's attention as she discussed
the grandkids
There was talk, all one sided of course, as she ask God to
watch over the great grandkids
Stepping up the pace she talked to God about the terrible things
happening in the world

I raised my own bowed head and looked at her out
of the corner of my eye
A tear drop had formed on her cheek as she talked to God
about the hungry kids
God must have spoken to her because a smile formed at
the corners of her mouth
And all at once there was a slight giggle as she said,
"Thanks God, I knew you would."

The prayer was ended, or so I thought, as she brushed away
some crumbs from her plate
"Oh, one more thing dear God" and she bowed her head once again
and looked upward

I forgot to thank you for the Irishman that you brought into my life a little while ago
I feel so loved and cared for and his corny jokes sure make me laugh, talk to you tomorrow.

Terrence Morrissey

High In The Sky

I saw an eagle soaring high in the sky
Once swooping toward the earth
And then next dashing toward the sun
A majestic bird on a majestic mission

Carrying a message of exotic love
Dipping across the meadows so grand
Touching the tree tops with wings outspread
Framed in the noonday sun, an outline of magnificence

On the eagle's wings a message for a lover
Holding fast as the wind rushed by
My heart was as the eagle's flight
Carrying a message of love high up in the sky

Terrence Morrissey

How Can I Say I Love You

I can say it in a song
Or with a bouquet of flowers
Or dinner in really nice restaurant
Or a special gift on a special day

But anyone can say I love you
In that old fashioned way
I mean I really love you
And I want you to know how much

So I think I will just love you
For all eternity and here is what I'll do
I will tell you that I love you
By all the things I do

I will be respectful and helpful too
I will always speak well of you no matter what
I will hold your hand when you are troubled
And I will always protect you no matter what

You can count on me to be where you need me to be
I will listen with patience when you have a need to talk
I will hold you close when pain has entered your heart
But most of all I will always just say "I love you" no matter what

By Terrence Morrissey

I Am Committed

I am a part of the fellowship of the unashamed. I have stepped over the line. The decision has been made. I will not look back, let up, slow down, back away, or be still.

My past is redeemed. My present makes sense. My future is secure. I am finished and done with low living, sight walking, small planning, smooth knees, colorless dreams, tamed visions, mundane talking, cheap living and dwarfed goals.

I no longer need preeminence, position or popularity. I don't have to be right. I don't have to be first. I don't have to be recognized. I don't have to be praised. I don't have to be regarded. I don't have to be rewarded.

I am committed to the Lord Jesus Christ. I now live by faith. I lean on His presence. I walk with patience. I live by prayer. I labor in love. My face is set. My road is narrow. My way is rough. My companions may be few, but my Guide is reliable. My mission is clear. I cannot be bought, deluded or delayed.

I will not flinch in the face of sacrifice. I will not hesitate in the presence of adversity. I will not negotiate at the table of the enemy. I will not meander in the maze of mediocrity. I won't give up. I won't shut up. I won't let up until I have stayed up, stored up, prayed up, paid up and preached up for the cause of Jesus Christ.

I am a disciple of the Lord Jesus. I will go till He comes. I will give till I drop. I will preach till all know. I will work till He stops me. And when

He comes, He will find faith and commitment in my life. When He returns, He will have no problem recognizing me.

Author Unknown

I Dreamed A Dream Of Love

I awoke one early morn; the moon was golden in the sky
I watched as stars sparkled and danced amongst the clouds
And a moonbeam cut a golden path across the heavens
I saw her smile as her eyes danced with laughter

The tree tops swayed in that gilded moment
And an early morning bird sang softly to the dawn
A heaven sent sound that made my heart glad
And in that song she once more smiled for me alone

Softly I heard her sigh as she nestled gently in my arms
The softness of her touch was as a gentle breeze
Caressing my very soul as my heart beat with a song of love
I dreamed a dream of love as I awoke with my beloved on my mind

Terrence Morrissey

I Guess

I guess I'll always love you
I guess it will be forever
I guess you broke my heart
I guess it will be broken forever

I guess the sun came up this morning
I guess it did not rise in my heart
I guess the clouds will always be there
I guess they will follow me forever

I guess the moon still shines at night
I guess it always will but not for me
I guess the flowers will always bloom
I guess they will never again bloom for me

I guess the birds will always sing
I guess they will but not in my heart
I guess I will always love you
I guess that you will never love me

I guess I will never forget your warm embrace
I guess I will never again feel your lips touch mine
I guess it might have all been a dream
I guess, I guess, I guess

Terrence Morrissey

I Know God Created You For Me

Spider webs in the trees,
Covered in water droplets
And shining in the sun
Silver droplets all aglow

A butterfly settled on a rose
A bumble bee gathering nectar
A humming bird and a merry tune
A swallow alight a heavenly tower

A song bird singing a song of love
A passionate heart sighs with joy
As I see a smile of love upon your face
Then I know God created you for me

Terrence Morrissey

I Loved You Once Before I Can Love You Once Again

Love came and captured their hearts
They were so young and so much in love
They spoke of a forever love and promised one another
To be forever true and always to be faithful too

The years came and the years flew by
The little ones arrived just as they had planned
Her heart was filled with the miracle of love
He worked hard and kept his promises true

Until that fateful day when another caught his eye
It all happened so fast it took them by surprise
He awoke one morn with another by his side
His heart was broken by what he had done

The divorce was quick and the pain was great
As his wife walked out the door with children in hand
He begged forgiveness for what he had done
Sadness was his constant companion day after day

Please, he pleaded, I know I broke my promise to be true
Her heart filled with forgiveness and with love felt his pain inside
The deepness of his sorrow was plain for all to see
She whispered…"I loved you once before, I can love you once again."

Terrence Morrissey

I Will Never Not Love You All The Days Of My Life

It is not because when I take your hand in mine
And my heart is overtaken with a love before unknown
It is not because when I look into your beautiful brown eyes
I lose my heart and for the love of you I scarce can breathe

It is not because when the sun arose one morn and a songbird sang
And I was moved with such emotion by your beautiful self
That I praise the day you were born and also praise the day we met
Lost in the tranquil beauty of your smile and the musical sound of
your voice

It is not because one early morn you awoke and whispered
that you loved me
And the remembrance of your embrace as you slept quietly
in my arms
And I saw a golden moonbeam caress the beauty of your sweet face
It is all of the above and even more that makes my heart declare

"I WILL NEVER NOT LOVE YOU
ALL THE DAYS OF MY LIFE"

Terrence Morrissey

I Will Never See

A sunrise as beautiful as the love I saw in your eyes
when first our eyes did meet
Nor will I ever see a sunset as calm and as sweet
As when I first saw you sleeping
No, never will I see an enchanted forest as lovely as you
when first I saw you smile
No, no, not ever will my eyes behold an angel
as divine nor as sweet as you.

Terrence Morrissey

If I Could Have My Way

If I could have my way
I would take you in my arms
And to the sound of heavenly music
I would waltz you into my heart

If I could have my way
I would walk with you at daybreak
With a rainbow as our path
Across a billowy sky

If I could have my way
And with our hearts beating as one
We would skip along the sun's golden rays
And dance in the light of a moonbeam

If I could have my way
I would make you mine forever
And waltz with you for eternity
Along heaven's Milky Way

If I could have my way

Terrence Morrissey

In The Garden Of My Heart

Sleepily, one morning, I saw a figure walking in my garden
She walked amongst a garden bouquet of flowers
Captivating were the flowers arrayed in a thousand colors
The figure, standing alone, was so much more beautiful

An enchanting fragrance slowly lifted to the sun
The figure, moving as in a dream, smiled an entrancing smile
A love song satisfied the morning quiet from a lone songbird
Alas the song of the shadowy figure was all the sweeter

The shadow, slightly turning, saw me gazing upon her beauty
Now smiling a smile of loveliness, cast over a disappearing shoulder
Vanished, as a song bird called, once again, among the flowers
In an instant my heart joined in a song of happiness

Terrence Morrissey

It Happened One Day

Today I held her in my arms
A tender, soft and gentle woman
A teardrop from the depth of her heart
Shone sadly upon her cheek

All at once gliding softly into my arms
As lovely and gentle as a baby in springtime
The fragrance 'round about her my heart did hold
And the love in her eyes spoke of a love renewed
It happened one day.

Terrence Morrissey

Just Ask

I tossed and turned in my darkened cave,
My body speared with deep despair:
I cursed those who had conspired so
To leave me, lonely there.

The entrance I had sealed myself
With anger, lies and pain,
My palms bloodied from the futile tries,
To open up that tomb again.

Nowhere to turn, no one to trust,
I had given up the task;
A whispered voice said "If you need help,
"All you have to do is ask."

I saw a slivered shaft of light,
Blaze between the cave and boulder;
A touch of hope that lifted me,
Strong hands upon my shoulder.

I dug deeper down, fell on my knees
Then remembered how to pray,
He put His hands on top of mine
And we rolled the rock away!

A mighty wind came rushing in
And stripped my body bare,
In the comfort of my sunshine
I was reborn and aware.

The rock was moved, my path revealed,
Not smooth, not straight, not wide;
But twists and turns and obstacles
That Him and I would take in stride.

"I've been so wrong; how do I repay
For this new life that you give?"
The winds were stilled, the world was quiet,
He said simply, "I Forgive!"

Jim McGregor
Easter 2000

Knowing True Love Once More

A whisper of a breeze touched the curl on her forehead
She smiled as though she held the happiness of the world in her heart
A sparkle like the sun bouncing off a diamond danced in her eyes
A spirit of love and peace encompassed the sweetness of her face

She held a single rose as a dew drop from off the petals
fell to the ground
The sound of a love song filled the air as the words touched
her very being
Words of love, happiness and joy entered upon her very soul
Alas, she spoke to the wind and the sun; this is my destiny to behold

Slowly walking across a carpet of grass she melted into
his outstretched arms
He was Irish with that wondrous Irish smile and
he held her hand in his
Holding her close to his breast, his arms gathered round 'bout her
Slowly ever slowly drawing her closer they embraced as lover always do

She rested her head upon his shoulder as he kissed that
curl upon her head
They spoke of love and of ecstasies yet to come as his lips touched hers
The single rose she held close to her breast burst open
with petals anew
They walked into a golden sunrise and she once more knew true love

Terrence Morrissey

Laughter And A Smile

It wasn't the way she entered a room
That caught the eye of every man
It wasn't the way she wore her clothes
That brought silence to the chamber

She entered that room with a gentle sway
And the smile that greeted that room full of folk
Was like a sunrise on a clear and beautiful morn
More lovely than a full golden moon kissing the tree tops

She looked at you with eyes that were a delicate blue
And your heart was imprisoned, captured forever
She spoke and your joy knew no bounds
How you blushed as she embraced your mind and soul

As she moved across the room all eyes were upon her
A sassy little walk with strands of golden hair thrown back
A glancing look in your direction with laughter and a smile
Sixteen months old she captured the heart of every of
everyone in the room

Terrence Morrissey

Life Or Death The Choice

The bar was dingy, the lights turned down low
Laughter from some corners, angry words from others
He sat and listened with sadness, anger and a solemn heart
Now the choice was his to make, another drink or the door

He stood to go but his legs were weak, his mind weaker still
Reaching the door he grabbed the handle, just one more step
But wait, the laughter and the loud voices drew him back
Sitting down he motioned to the waitress, the choice was his to make

As the waitress approached, his mind reeled with thoughts
of his family
The laughter around the house and the dinner table was no more
It was traded for anger, swearing, accusations, filth and disgust
The memory of a child's tears seared his troubled mind

The waitress stood and in a cold and detached voice asked,
"The usual?"
He nodded in the affirmative and watched her walk away
His mind whirled and he closed his fist, nails dug deep
as blood appeared
If he couldn't hit it, then he couldn't fix it or so he came to believe

Swaying, as he stood, he lurched toward the door and
the laughter was no more
Grabbing the handle he stumbled into the night, his mind and
soul determined
This pain must end, the insanity has to go, he thought as a star
shone overhead

Determination now gripped his mind as he walked away,
never looking back

Another door, he opened it with a smile and a bounce was in his step
There was laughter and loud talking but something was different
"You made a good choice when you chose life." his new friend spoke
"The choice between life and death." And his first AA meeting began

Terrence Morrissey

Living In A Dream

SHE ALWAYS WANTED TO BE IN LOVE
AT CHRISTMAS TIME
BUT TIME, CHANCE AND FATE HAD OTHER PLANS
FOR HER
SHE DREAMED AND DREAMED EVEN AS A LITTLE GIRL
THAT SOMETHING MAGIC WOULD HAPPEN AT THIS
TIME OF YEAR

EVERY CHRISTMAS THE TREE WAS DECORATED
LIGHTS ALL AGLOW
TINSEL HUNG ON EVERY BRANCH WITH LOVE AND
VERY MUCH CARE
NO MATTER HOW HARD SHE TRIED SHE COULDN'T
STOP THE TEARS
ANOTHER YEAR GONE BY AND THAT MAGIC LOVE DID
NOT APPEAR

SHE DIDN'T WANT OR NEED ANY GIFTS
BENEATH THE TREE
ALL SHE EVER PRAYED FOR WAS TO BE IN LOVE AT
CHRISTMAS TIME
SHE WAITED EACH CHRISTMAS EVE AS A TEAR
CARESSED HER CHEEK
BUT SANTA JUST SEEMED TO FORGET THAT LONELY
LITTLE GIRL

SHE STOOD BESIDE HIM AND AT ONCE
THEIR EYES DID MEET

SHE FELL IN LOVE AND HE DID ALSO, HOW MAGIC WAS
THIS THING
HE FILLED HER HEART WITH LOVE, AS SHE FILLED HIS
HEART WITH LOVE
THEY NOW SHARE THEIR LIVES TOGETHER EVERY DAY
OF THE YEAR

THEY SIT BENEATH A CHRISTMAS TREE AND LOVE HAS
HER IN ITS SPELL
WITH LOVE, LAUGHTER AND JOY THEY OPEN ALL
THEIR GIFTS
MEMORIES ARE CREATED EACH MOMENT ALL
THROUGH THE NIGHT
FOR SHE NOW LIVES HER DREAM AND IS IN LOVE AT
CHRISTMAS TIME

Terrence Morrissey
December 25th

Lost In The Beauty Of Your Smile

The roaring river held me spellbound
The cascading waterfall awakened a new longing
The mountain's volcano stirred me to a new life
The lightning bolt electrified my feelings

But absolutely nothing on earth or in the sky
Could move me, body soul or spirit
As the moment that I stood breathless
When looking into your beautiful brown eyes
My heart stood still....lost in the beauty of your smile

Terrence Morrissey

Love At Last Entwined

I'm so deeply in love with you
That I hardly know what to say
Just hoping you'll take my hand
And one day walk my way

An aching heart so full of hurt
Yet I know not which way to turn
As I watch you walk the other way
And I'm left with a painful longing

How beautiful you are, so sweet and fair
As the golden sunlight dances circles in your hair
The shadow of a cloud does frame your beautiful smile
And I am left wondering if you'll ever walk my way

To dream of your hand held gently in my own
Is almost more than I can bear but the dream lingers on
Maybe one day soon we'll walk together hand in hand
And I'll hear your sweet voice make my dream come true

When your lips touch mine and with a gentle kiss you place
With breathless anticipation and a smile so sweet and kind
Your hand in mine and love does flow from heart to heart
I hear you whisper, "I do" and at last our love entwined

Terrence Morrissey

Love Came And Broke My Heart

The creek was dry, barren it was
The lake was without water, how sad the sight
A river was spoiled, no fish lived there
And the ocean disappeared from across the earth

The hills held no flowers, not a single one bloomed
The meadow was without life, not a petal on the ground
The trees were unfruitful, nothing grew there
A lonely figure walked with head bowed down

No life existed, and all was for naught
Not a star in the sky, the nighttime told
The moon's golden glow was but a shadow
The sun never rose with a smile anymore

When all at once, into my life did appear
A woman so lovely that I was left breathless
Come, take my hand, she did express
And as in a dream I was at once alive

The creek that was barren flowed silently by
The lake without water was graceful and winding
In the river, the fish did swim silver tails aglow
The oceans of the world with new life did abound

We walked and laughed and smiled a smile of love
As we gazed deep into each other's heart and soul
I held her in my arms oh so very tight
As we clung to each other a tear from her eye did flow

We waltzed on the soft grass beneath our feet
The music that played was playing in our hearts
I never felt a love so complete, it was surely absolute
A lady standing nearby smiled a smile of understanding

Then all at once as from out of the tempest
The creek was once more barren
And the lake was without water
No life existed in the rivers and the oceans were no more

I walk at night but no stars are there
The gold of the moon has departed and left but a shadow
The sun does not rise to greet my heart with a smile
For my lover has left me with a tear drop in my heart

Terrence Morrissey

Love On The Wings Of A Dove

I saw a dove circling high in the sky
Once gliding toward the earth
And then next dashing toward the sun
A majestic bird on a majestic mission

Carrying a message of exotic love
Dipping across the meadows so grand
Touching the tree tops with wings outspread
Framed in the noonday sun, an outline of magnificence

On the wings of a dove, a message to my lover
Holding fast as the wind rushes by
I see my beloved and my heart is lifted on high
And it carries to her a message of love on the wings of a dove

Terrence Morrissey

Love Over The Telephone

One day, she told, she had a word with God
And told Him of the pain in her heart
She was lonely and feeling very blue
Would she ever find love again to still the pain within

Be patient, and have no fear was the reply that she heard
So she just decided to trust that voice and quiet her very soul
But every day it was there, this yearning to be loved
And to give love in return for this was the dream of one and all

She sat beside a stranger one day but something wasn't the same
He smiled at her and said 'hello' and she knew that it was special
Her heart did flutter, a happiness and longing felt deep within
She returned his smile and with blushing eyes she also said 'hello'

Today it happened and she told him that she loved him
And he replied that he was falling in love with her too
You could hear their hearts beating very loud and clear
And it all took place on a rainy afternoon…over the telephone

Terrence Morrissey

Memories At Twilight

WHEN ONCE WE SAT NEARBY THE SHORE
MEMORIES LINGER OF MY BELOVED AT THE DOOR
DRINKS IN HAND AND A WELCOMING SMILE
KNOWING FULL WELL WE WILL LINGER AWHILE

A DOE IN THE SHADOWS ALL PEACEFUL AND SERENE
KEEPING A WATCH ON THE TWO LOVERS DOWN BY
THE SHORE
NOW THE CHAIRS STAND EMPTY AND THE
TABLE IS BARE
THE TIDE ON THE WAY OUT SO TOO ARE THE
MEMORIES AT TWILIGHT

NOW THE LOVERS SIT ON A HEAVENLY SHORE
AS A CHORUS OF ANGELS SING A SONG OF LOVE
THE SMILE STILL LINGERS AND THEIR
FINGERS ENTWINE
A MEMORY MADE AT TWILIGHT AS HE SPOKE "WILL
YOU BE MINE"

SHE ANSWERED WITH WORDS OF ENDEARING LOVE
AND LIFETIME OF BLISS AT THAT TABLE BY THE SHORE
BONDED TWO LOVERS NEVER MORE TO PART
MEMORIES AT TWILIGHT FOREVER MORE

Terrence Morrissey

Miles Between Us

I walk the floor each night, thinking of you
Hoping to hear footsteps outside my bedroom door
But alas, the silence of the night is deafening
As I think of distance and the miles between us

I hear the sounds of the traffic in the street
I hear the chatter of the folks as they pass on by
The laughter of the crowd does not my longing erase
As I think of the distance and the miles between us

A nightingale stirs memories within as it sings a song of love
A lonely moonbeam, through an open window
Makes a path across my bedroom floor and my heart does stir
As I think of the distance and the miles between us

Dawn breaks with a crimson red and yellow sky
A rainbow appears in the distance with colors all aglow
But the night has vanished, I spent another night alone
As I think of the distance and the miles between us

Terrence Morrissey

My Beloved, My Piano And Me

The room was large like an enormous ballroom
The walls were white, a beautiful angelic white
The sun filtered with brilliance through lace curtains,
As comforting shadows swayed gently to the music

My beloved's favorite song softly filled the air
And was mellow beneath my ever moving finger tips
As I caressed the smooth white ivory of the piano
A teardrop on my cheek, I was sure that she had smiled

My love of fifty years or more lay still upon her bed
Her eyes were closed and her countenance sweet
And the beauty of yesteryear was calm upon her face
Did she hear the music, I reflected as I played

They came shortly thereafter, those folks all dressed in white
And wheeled her bed across that immense hospital room
Out the swinging doors she went not conscious of a thing
I played on until the dusk, then and closed the piano down

Walking through those swinging doors I heard an angel say
Wipe the tear from your eye for today she really heard you play
In the future, not so far away, I will once again hear her laughter
But for the present all alone I sit and play her favorite song

They buried my beloved today and as the silence rang
I could hear the angels singing as she danced among the clouds
A smile upon her face as she waits for me to play her favorite song,
Alone together once more, my beloved, my piano and me

*For my good friend Doug Armstrong reminiscing about the last days of his dear wife.
Thank you for your friendship and allowing me to put your feelings into words.

Terrence Morrissey
Copyright June 6, 2011

My Chair

I have a weekly meeting
And lots of folks come there;
I have to get there early
To be sure to get MY CHAIR.

Now there is always lots of seating
But so that everyone understands,
If you touch MY CHAIR, my friend,
I'll probably slap your hands.

It is strategically located
So I can hear with my good ear,
Its six steps from the coffee pot
And the sandwiches are near.

I have a sightline for the bathroom
And the path is clear and wide,
The door is right behind me,
A quick exit to outside.

I've learned tolerance and forgiveness
And how to make amends,
But you just leave MY CHAIR alone,
And we can still be friends.

You can come there if you want to,
There is always comfort there,

But sit beside or behind me
Just don't sit in MY CHAIR!

Jim McGregor

My Heart Was On Every Ride

I asked her if I could kiss her, as I looked into her big brown eyes
Her rosy red lips were so inviting I just couldn't help myself
She smiled a shy but teasing smile as she replied, "Oh heavens no."
The room is much too crowded and people
will really never understand

Smiling a modest but alluring smile she turned her cheek to my lips
Just a simple kiss, said she, as I kissed her soft and lovely cheek
But my heart wanted so much more, my heartache was quite apparent
Easy does it, and go very, very slow were the words that she uttered

With surprise and awe I took a step back and here is what I said
Can a man at the top of a roller coaster ride demand the ride to go
very, very slow
Or at the height of a turbulent white water ride expect to
say, easy does it
Or a cowboy riding a raging bull say to the bull, easy does it,
go very, very slow

My heart was on a roller coaster ride while sitting on a raging bull and
riding a raging wave
Take it easy and go very, very slow....absolutely impossible...and here
is the reason why
Just stay off the roller coaster and don't get on that bull, and really
avoid the raging rapids
But when she took my hand in her hand I knew it was too late....my
heart was on every ride

Terrence Morrissey

My Last True Love

Was it the sinking crimson sun beyond the horizon
Or was it the last flower of summer
Possibly it was the sigh of a baby as it drifted off to sleep
Maybe it the last sight of a waterfall as the morning mist engulfed it

Could it be the beauty of a full golden moon as it first peeked above
the horizon?
Just maybe, it was the first flower of springtime opening alone upon a
mountain top
I know, it is the early morning giggle of a baby discovering its toes for
the first time
It surely must have been the cascading water as the early morning
dams are opened

As I contemplate the sinking sun beyond the horizon and the last
flower of summer
And as I contemplate the sigh of a baby drifting off to sleep and a
misty morning waterfall
I see clearly the majesty of a full golden moon and the blossoming of
spring's first flower
Now it is the cascading water, as the flood gates are opened, that I
think upon

And putting all this together I am mindful of my love for you when
first we met
The flower did bloom, the water did flow, the sun peeked at the hori-
zon and a baby giggled
And then I thought of the sunset of my life and the last flower
of my summer

Which of these would I choose to gaze upon before
being lifted to eternity
I can have them all by seeing, at my last, your sweet face before me,
For you hopefully, will be my last and only true love

Terrence Morrissey

My Love For You Is........

Ocean deep, mountain high
Meadow wide, rainbow beautiful
Unyielding as a silvery moon
Dazzling as the morning sunshine
Sparkling as an ocean wave in the moonlight
Glittering as a cluster of stars on a starlit night
Stronger than the mightiest wind
Longer lasting than all eternity

Dedicated to your happiness forever
Comforting when you are sad
Strong when weakness overtakes you
Gentle when you need a gentle touch
Caring when the trials of life overpower you
Careful always of your innermost feelings
Faithfully by your side when you feel threatened
Contented when I know you are happy

Terrence Morrissey

My Lover And My Friend

She's said she was my lover
But she's also my very best friend
Whenever she holds my hand
She holds my heart there too

Her lips touched mine one fine sunny morn'
As I reeled from the encounter I felt I was just reborn
Looking deep within her beautiful blue eyes
I caught a glimpse of something there

What I saw would surprise anyone or so it seems
For I saw an angel dancing there
Behind those beautiful blue eyes
That Angel danced a dance of love for my lover and my friend

Terrence Morrissey

My One And Only

The sun was rising and so were the birds
My heart rose up and greeted the day
My blessings were multiplied
When I saw where you lay

Right there beside me all serene and lovely
Was the woman I love, so full of goodness
Calmness and beauty all rolled into one
An angel is my beloved, how happy I am

Thank you for loving me and holding me close
Thank you for being so special in the eyes of God
Thank you for allowing me a glimpse of your heart
Thank you for being my one and only, never to part

Terrence Morrissey

Needing God

I AWOKE THIS MORNING OUT OF A DEEP SLEEP
BEFORE THE BIRDS BEGAN THEIR
EARLY MORNING TRILL
MY HEART WOULD NOT BE STILL,
NOT EVEN FOR A MOMENT
MY BEATING HEART STARTLED EVEN THE SILENCE
OF THE MORN

AS A DEW DROP NEEDS AN EARLY MORNING ROSE
AS A FISH NEEDS A MOVING SPARKLING RIVER
AS A BIRD ON THE WING NEEDS A
GENTLY SWAYING BREEZE
SO DOES MY HEART NEED GOD, SO IT ALSO CAN
BEGIN TO SING

Terrence Morrissey

Never No Never

You say that you love me and how I love to hear you say it
It leaves me with a feeling of being wanted, loved and cherished
You tell me that you miss me whenever we are apart
How I love to hear those words that make me feel so treasured

Now, my precious darling, I too can say I love you and
love you I truly do
I love you with an undying love that forever will be unforgettable
I miss you, my treasurable and adorable darling and miss you endlessly
When you put your hand in mine I can feel the depth of our
love for each other

I awake each morning greeted by your tender smile
The softness of your body is as velvet to my touch
Your beating heart is as the sound of a morning songbird
As it sings a melody of love that embraces my whole being

I could search the whole world over and stand upon a mountain top
I could look in the deepest jungles and explore the oceans clear
I could search the heavens and count the stars above
Never, no never, my beloved could I ever find love as precious as yours

Terrence Morrissey

Not So Long Ago

I saw you walking in the pale moonlight

And the rose you planted in the garden of my heart

When once we were lovers, blushed a thoughtful blush

Watered by the tears of a broken heart

The rose lives on

Terrence Morrissey

One Rainy Morning

I walked into her little delicatessen
And saw her standing there
In a pretty blue dress and apron too
It all happened one rainy morning

"Hi" she said with a voice tender and kind
"Hello, I replied with a strange feeling in my heart
"Would you like a coffee"? The voice of an angel said
"It all happened one rainy morning

I stood to go and she came and stood before me
"See you again soon, I hope" her lovely eyes said
"My world and my heart stood still, as I kissed her lips
It all happened one rainy morning

Terrence Morrissey

Only Because

You are absolutely wonderful, marvellous and beautiful
And anyone can understand why
A magnificent mother, grandmother and GREAT grandmother
Enjoy your day knowing that God loves you and is so
very proud of you.

Terrence Morrissey

Peace And Joy

Let peace and joy be your companion today and forever more. Seek only that which creates a calmness within you and allows the sunshine of those that love you be forever a companion to your heart and spirit.

The morning broke upon a mountain so grand
Flowers coming alive at the kiss of the sun
The morning mist gently engulfed a beautiful spirit
A gentle wind caressed the sweetness of her soul

She embraced the morning as a mother embraces a newborn child
And held her head high, walking hand in hand with her Lord
Be calm, a voice within heart did speak, and know not fear
For today you are loved and kindness is your companion

You are loved, much more than you can know
The sweetness within your heart and spirit
Makes your lover's heart aglow
As he wakes in the early morn and embraces you

Now smile, a smile of Peace and Joy
And listen as the early morning songbirds sing
They sing a song of happiness for you and for you alone
As an angel smiles and caresses your heart with love.

Terrence Morrissey

Pink Shoes

I first heard the gentle steps approaching from behind
Turning I looked down and that was when I first saw her
A gracious and pleasant smile standing in
The Pink Shoes

How cute, I thought as my eyes wandered
First the ankles, how tiny and smooth they were
And then long slim legs, but my eyes wandered back to
The Pink Shoes

A voice as sweet as honeycomb spoke gently
Hi, she spoke, and her emerald blue eyes
Danced a flirting dance as I looked once again at
The Pink shoes

Strawberry blonde hair caught in a gentle breeze
As she looked out from behind a veil of softness
I could scarcely breathe as I beheld the beauty of
The Pink Shoes

I am perplexed as I contemplate
Why anyone would wear pink shoes
To take out the trash.

Terrence Morrissey

Poetry And Love

Poetry is not written about love

But rather about the memory of love

Of loving and being loved

Of hearing a songbird at twilight

Of melting into a lover's arms

Capturing, in a heartbeat

The most beautiful part of love

That intimate moment

When love meets love

And memories are forever made

Terrence Morrissey

Six Short Weeks

It was only six short weeks ago
That you walked into my heart
I seem to think it has been forever
My memories of yesteryear, I cannot recall

Your love entered like a rushing gentle wind
Riding on a rainbow of tenderness
Captivating was your smile
As you looked deep within my soul

Surely you found what you had been longing for
As certainly as did I when first you entered in
The touch of your hand as you took mine
Sent volumes of love letters that touched my very being

The honeymoon had begun with love and laughter
As we embraced and promised to love forever
I glance and there you are sleeping with a smile upon your face
And to think it all began just six short weeks ago

Terrence Morrissey

Spellbound Forever

YOU ARE SO VERY BEAUTIFUL
AND SO LOVELY TO LOOK AT
YOU LEAVE ME BREATHLESS
WHENEVER I LOOK UPON YOUR FACE

THE GENTLENESS OF YOUR TOUCH
THE SWEET CARESS OF YOUR SMILE
AS YOU WALK INTO MY ARMS
WILL HOLD ME SPELLBOUND FOREVER

Terrence Morrissey

Standing In The Noon Day Sun

I saw her standing in the noonday sun
As a gentle breeze kissed her wine colored lips
Her cheeks aglow were also gently caressed
And the breeze tenderly shifted her golden locks

Captured in a moment of time my heart did yield
Love sprung forth as a surging tide held in endless wonder
Seized by a beauty so unique that my heart stood in silent awe
What now, cried the spirit of love within me, what now?

The noonday sun turned to a crimson sunset
As we strolled, hand in hand by a lake of blue
A golden moon smiled at a beauty so rare indeed
Hearts entrapped and held captive for time without end

A teasing bewitching kiss as a song bird sang a song of love
A caressing glance into her dancing eyes
Found my heart reaching to embrace her heart
And our hearts embraced while standing in the noonday sun

Terrence Morrissey

The Battlefield Of Life
A True Champion

Born to fight, to win and never lose
Life moved on and age did grow
Life became a battlefield just like a title fight
Fifteen rounds by the time the battle was won

Memories sought out the mind like a plague
An old oak tree gently swaying in the breeze
A lone bird sitting on a branch smiling at the wind
But round one in the battle of life had not yet begun

A childhood filled with happy sounds of laughter and chuckles
With friends to share a story with, some bringing painful tears
Days and nights filled with awe as life was learned in amazement
Sitting alone atop a hill with the rolling wind
caressing a curious smile

A little bird came by one day and didn't see anyone sitting there
Looking at the lord's creation that bird was as enchanted as could be
A little movement, a whispered sound and that little bird
turned to stare
That little bird sure was surprised, to see alcohol sitting there

But alas as the years flew by it was time to stand and
face the trials of life
Those trials were a mighty surprise and were overwhelming with
panic and dread

Now it was round one in this heavyweight fight and so-
briety came out swinging
The first round was lost, but up got sobriety to face round two and
three and more

The battle was fierce and quite a few rounds were lost but again he
got back on his feet
Facing his opponent on this battlefield of life he found himself de-
feated again and again
Round ten was filled with the opponent, alcohol, taking its toll on this
battered one
Then round eleven and all seems lost and bewilderment became the
enemy in that round

Round twelve and the foe was crafty with lies and promises that no
one could resist
Then a gleam of hope and sparkle did take over to
everyone's admiration
Round thirteen did take its toll but he refused to quit,
got up again and again
Round fourteen, the crowd was on its feet, he was still fighting this
battle for life

The last round, bloody and messy it was, but alcohol was
on the ropes at last
A desire for sobriety came out swinging with resolve of mind in this
battle for life
The crowd stood cheering as God raised sobriety's hand in victory
On this battlefield called life, there stood sobriety, the winner by a
Knock Out

Terrence Morrissey

The Day God Smiled

Early one morning God stretched forth His hand
He looked upon the sunrise He had created.
Seeing through eternity He pondered what He had created
A songbird alighted on His outstretched palm....

God could not smile....something is missing, thought He
He looked at the creation of His first flower
It stood alone in a sweet fragrant meadow
Looking, the Lord saw the sunrise and then He saw the sunset

He was well pleased with the beauty of the two....
But alas thought the Lord ....something is missing.
God then placed a rainbow in the sky
And there was rejoicing at the beauty that greeted His eyes....

But something was missing and God could not smile
He then created the sun, moon and stars
At this beauty the birds began to sing a song of praise
God was well pleased but still no smile adorned His face.

Early one morning as God stretched forth His hand
Heaven and earth rejoiced with songs at the beauty that
God had created
They all asked, "What will you call this, your most
beautiful creation?"
God pondered the question and with a happy heart He said,

"I will call this beautiful creation, woman," and God smiled.

Terrence Morrissey

The Day You Walked Back

I watched you walk away and you promised you would be back
I waited and watched for you every single day
The days flew by and the clock never stopped
I just kept praying for the day you walked back

The days turned into weeks and the weeks into months
But I never stopped watching, waiting and hoping
As the clock kept ticking and time kept passing
My heart hoped and yearned for the day you walked back

The sun rose early in the morning as it always did
And the moon soon after embracing the evening mist
I paced the floor both day and night
Always watching for the day you walked back

I remember it clearly as I lay upon this bed
The years have come and gone, I can scarce raise my head
They handed me a letter and this is what it said
It said that you had died the day you walked away
And now I lay me down in peace a smile upon my face
For I never shall see the day that you walked back

Terrence Morrissey

The Evening Sky

It was twilight when I first heard the song
Sweet sounding and gentle to my ear
The beauty of the song caressed my heart
And I saw your loveliness deep within that song

It was twilight and the sun was fading into a western sky
Crimson red with hues of blue and amber touching the evening sky
I saw your smile in the twilight as a restful breeze caressed your lips
My heart wept a tear of joy as I thought of the twilight of our love

Deep within this heart of mine a caressing love was sown
Gently there began to bloom the first petals of love's sweet song
I feel your embrace as the twilight embraces the evening
Crimson red with hues of blue and amber touching the evening sky

Terrence Morrissey

The Gal With The Beautiful Eyes

Her name is sincerity and her eyes, a delightful light brown
Sparkled with a tinge of green and gold
Her smile is as pretty as a blossom at the first hint summer
Her laughter is as delightful as an early morning songbird

Strolling along the beach with a love song in her heart
Sincerity was guided by the light of the last star of the night
And greeted the rising of an early morning sun
The song in her heart grew lovelier as she thought of her lover

Holding her close to his heart with arms so strong
They were lovers in the golden glow of a heavenly moonlight
Embracing they heard a heavenly chorus sing a song of love
He whispered I love you and a night bird sang a song of love

Breathlessly and eagerly she whispered that she loved him too
Thus the gal with the beautiful eyes found her first true love
Her beautiful eyes twinkled in the shadow of a moonlit night
And shooting stars wrote sincerity's name across the heavens

Terrence Morrissey

The Girl That I Love

The Girl that I love is wild and beautiful
Strong and tender, happy and sad

The girl that I love has eyes of blue
Soft and gentle with a winning smile

The girl that I love purrs like a kitten
When cradled in my loving arms

The girl that I love has stolen my heart
And cares for it ever so tenderly

The girl that I love is mine forever
And I am hers, 'til death do us part

Terrence Morrissey

The Hug

I walked into the room one miserable day
And I heard some people say hey, it's good to see you today
Grab a chair and a coffee too, we'd like you to stay
With coffee in hand I stayed out of their way

Well I sat in the corner and kept an eye on them all
They talked about good times and bad times too
But mostly they talked about the day they first arrived
It saved my life, one was heard to say and mine too another one spoke

Ok, so what's the secret I was thinking to myself
That made them so darn happy that their laughter filled the hall
Half dead on Monday and alive on Tuesday, it just didn't make sense
I went back out another one said, well welcome back was
the chorus I heard

And on it went for almost an hour with lots of laughs and
a few tears too
But tears seemed to strengthen the lot as they joked about this and
joked about that
By golly I said to myself at the end, this is the place to find
a good friend
I stood to go and they did too but I couldn't get out
without a hug or two

Keep coming back were the words that I heard and sincere it was of
that I was sure
I'll come back, I said with surprise because today I met the cure for
my disease

I'll live another day I thought and made my way out the door with the
sign that said AA
It was the hug that did it and I knew it for sure, I'll be back for more I
said with a smile

Terrence Morrissey

The Kiss

I SAW A RAIBOW IN THE SKY
I FELT A GENTLE BREEZE UPON MY LIPS
THE FEELING OF SOFTNESS THAT I FELT
WAS AS A BUTTERFLY SETTLING UPON A ROSE
AND I KNEW THAT YOUR LIPS HAD TOUCHED MINE

Terrence Morrissey

The Love Of God Is Greater By Far

Than tongue or pen can ever tell;
It goes beyond the highest star,
And reaches to the lowest hell;
The guilty pair, bowed down with care,
God gave His Son to win;
His erring child He reconciled,
And pardoned from his sin
Oh, love of God, how rich and pure!
How measureless and strong!
It shall forevermore endure—
The saints' and angels' song.
When years of time shall pass away,
And earthly thrones and kingdoms fall,
When men who here refuse to pray,
On rocks and hills and mountains call,
God's love so sure, shall still endure,
All measureless and strong;
Redeeming grace to Adam's race—
The saints' and angels' song.
Could we with ink the ocean fill,
And were the skies of parchment made,
Were every stalk on earth a quill,
And every man a scribe by trade;
To write the love of God above
Would drain the ocean dry;
Nor could the scroll contain the whole,
Though stretched from sky to sky.

Author: The original was written by an inmate in an insane asylum hundreds of years ago. Some lines and music were subsequently added by others down through the years.

The Most Beautiful Day Of My Life

A beautiful and lovely child as most new babies are
But there was really something different this time
His mother had waited for so many long, long years
Daily prayers and wishful thinking really took their toll

All around her were lady friends of years and years
Each one, in turn, giving birth at the appointed time
Not me, she thought out loud and her prayers continued
Why not me God? She asked as another friend gave birth

Tears were her constant companion, her prayers never ceased
Maybe one day God would bless her with a child of her own
The years came and the years went by, but that little prayer remained
How she longed to have a baby, a child she could call her own

Then one night she heard from God and made a very bold move
Turning to her husband in the middle of the night she told him
of her prayer
The marriage bed was honored and for once love did abound
Only a short time later her discovery was tolled throughout the land

I'm pregnant, she shouted to one and all my God has not forsaken me
I'm blessed beyond measure and here I am right into my later years
The days were long and sometimes hard to bear the nights
were longer still
With a smile the new mom did exclaim "This is the most beautiful
day of my life."

On this day her new born baby did arrive, a beautiful child so it
has been said
The years have come and the years have gone, now her prayer
has changed
Mom gives thanks to God each day for not forgetting her wish,
for on this day
She still exclaims, with a beautiful smile and a happy heart

"This is the most beautiful day of my life."

Terrence Morrissey

The Night The Stars Came Alive

We woke in the very early morning
And looked up at the stars
They winked at us, or so it seemed
They spoke of a flawless love

I saw your smile in each and every one
I saw your love light in every star
As I see the love light in your eyes

She's mine, my heart silently sings
And I'm overcome with happiness
And I reach out to touch a star
As I reach out to touch her body

And I feel her loving warmth beside me
And my heart begins to rejoice
Soon she will turn to face me, so speaks my heart
As surely as the stars come alive each night

Silently in the stillness of the night
The stars appeared that sparkle in the night
And dreaming dreams of days gone by
Our hearts soar like eagles on the wing

While making love beneath the moon
A ray of gold kisses her on the cheek
And our hearts begin to rejoice
When the stars come alive each night

Terrence Morrissey

The Nurse

A Soldier, a Sailor and an Airman
Stood before the Pearly gates
Their faces were scarred and old
They stood before the man of fate
To be admitted to the fold

Saint Peter said what have you done,
To gain admittance here?
Said the Airman, I flew on many sad missions
And cried as my best friend hit the ground

Said the Sailor, I sailed a wide vast ocean
And fought amid the fire and rain
I watched as my buddy died
With a victory smile upon his face

Spoke up the soldier, with sadness in his voice
I fought in the trenches sir, with my buddies young and old
I saw them take their last breath
knowing their story would be told

The Pearly Gates swung open
Saint Peter rang the bell
Come in he said, to one and all, as a chorus of angles sang
For you've spent your time in hell

Then standing there with a smile upon her face
Was an old but beautiful woman
Waiting to be admitted to the fold

What have you done Saint Peter said
To gain admittance here?

Why I was a nurse and helper sir to all the brave above
I wiped their tears, and covered their wounds
I wept as I held the hand of many a mother's dying son
As he pleaded, please don't let go of my hand

The Pearly gates swung open
Saint Peter rang the bell as all heaven began to rejoice
Come in he said to the one with a heart so scarred
For you've spent your time in hell

Terrence Morrissey

The Only Thing That Kept Me From You

The only thing that kept me from you
That kept me from wrapping my arms around you
From feeling the warmth of your body close to mine
From feeling your heart beat as we lay naked upon the bed

The only thing that kept me from kissing your sweet lips
And from caressing your velvety smooth skin
From kissing you a thousand times and then a thousand times more
Was the presence of your little dog as he bit me on the rear

Terrence Morrissey

The Park Bench And A Stray Dog

He was asleep under the park bench, alone and forgotten
The night was cold and the park empty except for that stray dog
The falling rain beat a melody on the bench and soothed his weary soul
He was just eighteen years but looked sixty and sadness was on his face

The color drained from his face for the drugs had taken their toll
All the promises of youth were no more the dreams were long gone
It will make you happy, strong and peaceful, so he was told
Just stick this needle in your arm and your troubles will be no more

A broken home a drunken dad a cheating mother was all that he knew
No food on the table, another hungry night and
the pain was hard to bear
No father's arms around him, no mother's comforting love,
just a weary soul
I can make it on my own and he slipped out the window
into the rainy night

Just stick this needle in your arm and the promise sounded true
It was sharp and in a minute the dirty deed was done
They became his father and some became his mother
The love and warmth that overtook his soul was more than he ever had

Tonight, once again under the familiar bench with the rain upon his face
The fading color of his skin told the story very loud and clear
There would be no tomorrow no father's love no mother's yearning
He died there where he lay, a stray dog soothing his weary soul

Terrence Morrissey

The Promise

It was his first night on death row in a maximum security prison
He turned his face to the wall and wept bitter and repentant tears
The pain in his mind was surpassed only by the pain in his heart
A loving wife and two beautiful children left behind

The crime was a crime of passion and he knew he was wrong
Dead wrong as soon he shall be, dangling at the end of a rope
His mind dictated his words and his words dictated his actions
His actions revealed the character that was within and a man lay dead

Another man awaiting the noose lay on his bunk in the next cell
He heard the tears and he felt the pain of the young man as he cried
Leaning on one elbow he whispered in a voice of compassion
Young man, you must be courageous and try not to shed those tears

I am lost, the youngster cried in despair, I am lost for I know not God
I will teach you to pray said the other for I once was just like you
How was it you learned to pray whispered the youngster?
In the morning when you arise look out your cell window
said the other

A beam of sunlight blinded the young man's eyes in the early morn
He awoke as in a dream knowing the nightmare had just begun
The one destined for death in the cell across smiled as he awoke
to a new day
The young man glanced out his tiny window and a meadow
came into view

"What is that building?" He asked the older man across the
cold cement floor
It is a Christian church, he answered and I hear their
service every Sunday
That is how I learned to pray, he continued, just listening
to them folks in church
Now I will teach you how to pray as I learned it from
those folks every Sunday

Please do, cried the young man, please teach me how to pray like
those folks pray
Just bow your head and be as brave as can be and fear for nothing his
new friend said
Now believe this promise of God as I heard it every Sunday coming
from that happy Church
I will and he repeated what he was told…."God please forgive me" and
the lesson began

"For God so loved the world that He gave His only begotten son
That whosoever should believe in Him will not perish but will have
eternal life."
"I believe the promise" the doomed youngster cried and he heard a
voice from God
"You are forgiven; soon you will be with me in Paradise, no more pain
and no more suffering"

Terrence Morrissey

The Road Is Long

The road is long and very steep
Longer than I thought it would be
My burden is heavy and hard to carry
Heavier than I thought it would be

The journey has broken my heart
And the steepness has bent my spirit low
I never thought I would live to see it through
Longer than I thought it would be

The tears I shed spoke of an endless pain
Pieces of a broken heart strewn along the way
An ache so intense that I scarce could breath
More intense than I thought it would be

The sweat upon my brow is cold
The sun upon my face is unfriendly
Each step on this road called life is unfeeling
More unfeeling than I thought it would be

Terrence Morrissey

The Senior Entertainer

Senior entertainers are ordinary people
Doing extraordinary things
And they delight in the challenge
No obstacle is so huge
That they cannot overcome it
They have courage that others only dream of
In their eye is a determined glint
That says to the world
"Step aside, I have a job to do."

Terrence Morrissey

The Songbird

The billowy white clouds waved gently from the sky
As they gently drifted in a sky of heavenly blue
The Princess raised her eyes in wondrous amusement
As a songbird lighted upon a bouquet of beautiful flowers

Smiling and humming a song of delight against a sky so blue
The Princess raised an enchanted hand and caught the songbird
Looking deeply into her eyes he sang a song that said I love you
The Princess smiled a smile of delight and felt her heart flutter

The clouds sailed by, the sun began to set and evening was nigh
She held that songbird in her hand, a tear drop upon her cheek
Memories of yesteryear crowded the mind of the pretty Princess
As a new song and a new love embraced her sweet heart

Terrence Morrissey

The Sound Of Your Voice

I hear the sound of your sweet voice and your softly spoken words
As I tread the heavenly fields of clover soft beneath my feet
When at last one day you will appear on the horizon of my heart
And a chorus of angelic voices will welcome you home

There will be rejoicing, laughter and tears as you whisper 'I do'
Knowing at last, forever we will never more be parted
I will be your true love and adore you for all eternity
We will kiss a heavenly kiss beside a beguiling waterfall

As the first flower of the morning is kissed by a gentle breeze
Your lips kissed mine and once again I was lost in your loveliness
Suddenly we hear a song sounding gentle and lovely as in a dream
A song heard only in our hearts, placed there by the hand of God

The sparkle in your eyes and the laughter in your smile
Has once again captured my heart and soul for all eternity
Two hearts entwined, waltzing across a majestic rainbow
Your sweet voice whispers "I love you" as a songbird sings
a song of love

Terrence Morrissey

The Sun Was Rising

The sun was rising and so were the birds
My heart rose up and greeted the day
My blessings were multiplied
When I saw where you lay

Right there beside me all serene and lovely
Was the woman I love, so full of goodness
Calmness and beauty all rolled into one
An angel is my beloved, how happy I am

Thank you for loving me and holding me close
Thank you for being so special in the eyes of God
Thank you for allowing me a glimpse of your heart
Thank you for being my one and only, never to part

Terrence Morrissey

The Sweetest Words
I've Ever Heard

There is sweetness in the air when you take my hand in yours
There is the sweet sound of a nightingale as it sings a love song
There is the sweet fragrance of the first flowers of springtime
There is sweetness as a dew drop kisses the first flower
of the morning

But the sweetest sound that ever befell my ears,
Was the sound of your sweet voice echoing in my heart
When at the midnight hour and all the world was still
You raised your sweet head from off your pillow

And in the depth of your sweet and beautiful eyes
I saw there a love that was newly born as you took my hand in yours
And as you cuddled your sweet and tender body next to mine
I heard you whisper "I love you" the sweetest words I've ever heard

Terrence Morrissey

The Voice Of An Angel

In a dreamlike trance I heard an angel speak
Softly, gently, beguiling and inviting
My heart stopped, or so it seemed
And I heard a host of angels singing

What manner of heaven is this spoke my heart
For I am bewitched, enchanted and captivated
A sound so sweet that even the birds stopped singing
And paid rapturous attention to a voice so lovely

In an instant I awoke and looking around me
I realized that I had been bewitched and charmed
By the voice of an angel speaking a heavenly language
With a sound like a gentle summer's breeze

By Terrence Morrissey

The Wave Upon The Shore

LYING NAKED BENEATH A SHIMMERING MOON
THE NAKED LADY SIGHED
AS A MEMORY TOUCHED HER MIND
IN A PLACE SUCH AS THIS

FOR NOT SO MANY YEARS AGO
HER LOVER TOOK HER IN HIS ARMS
THEIR BODIES EMBRACED WITH A LOVE
THAT PROMISED TO NEVER END

A FEELING OF SOARING ABOVE HERSELF
AND LOOKING DOWN AS A THOUSAND DAYS
FLEETINGLY PASSED BEFORE HER VERY EYES
LET THIS NEVER END THE NAKED LADY DID SIGH

THE WARMTH OF A WAVE GENTLY TOUCHED
HER TOES
AS THE OCEAN BEGAN ITS RITUAL CRAWL
ACROSS A THOUSAND OCEANS AND UP UPON
THE LAND
SLOWLY, EVER SLOWLY, GENTLY EVER SO GENTLY

SHE WAS ONCE AGAIN EMBRACED BY HER LOVER
THE NAKED LADY AWAKENED
AND WITH A SIGH THAT HUSHED THE NIGHT
THE NAKED LADY KNEW

THAT THE DREAM SHE DREAMED
SHE WOULD DREAM NO MORE
FOR HER LOVER WAS ONLY
THE WAVE UPON THE SHORE

By Terrence Morrissey

Then There Were None*

First they came for the Communists
And I did not speak out
Because I was not a Communist;
Then they came for the Socialists
And I did not speak out
Because I was not a Socialist;
Then they came for the trade unionists
And I did not speak out
Because I was not a trade unionist;
Then they came for the Jews
And I did not speak out
Because I was not a Jew;
Then they came for me...
And there was no one left
To speak out for me.

*Pastor, Martin Niemoller wrote the above from a concentration camp

There Is No Bond So Sweet

THERE IS NO BOND SO SWEET
AS THE BOND OF LOVE
THAT TIES OUR HEARTS AS ONE

Terrence Morrissey

There Was A Moment

There was a moment when love was born from out of nowhere
There was a moment when a rainbow circled the heavens
There was a moment when a cascading river rushed to the ocean
There was a moment when a white rose bloomed on a mountain top

There was a moment when the sunshine greeted a new born baby
There was a moment when tear drops gathered on a young girl's cheek
There was a moment when a lover's smile made the whole world right

There was a moment when a raindrop kissed the first
flower of springtime
There was a moment when a baby doe peeked, in awe,
from behind a tree
There was a moment when a mother lay down her life
to protect her child
There was a moment when a young man died to bring
freedom to you and I

There was a moment when we all stared in amazement at the
miracle of birth
There was a moment when the world stood by as an unborn baby
was slaughtered
There was a moment when the elderly were dismissed
as having no value
There was a moment when darkness became a veil over the hearts
of mankind

There was a moment when there were no more tears and
compassion was lost

There was a moment when the ultimate in love and
compassion was dismissed
There was a moment when perfect love was cast from earth,
and the world wept
That moment was when they crucified perfect love, Jesus,
the son of God

Terrence Morrissey

.

There's A Freshness In The Air

There's a freshness in the air
There is beauty all around
Loveliness surrounds me
With every breath I take

More beautiful than a rose in bloom
Gilded love in every word she speaks
A stunning sunset is left wanting
Like a rose smiling as it blooms

A rising moon across still waters
A golden pathway reaching out
To embrace the splendor of her loveliness
They call her a lady....I call her adorable

Turning her head, a smile enchanted
Lips parted, her laughter consumes me
As I watch her turn and face the world
Sensually touchable as she walks away

Terrence Morrissey

They Call Her Great Grandmother

They call he great because she is a great grandmother
They call her great because she is a great cook
They call her great because she was and is a great mother
They call her great because she greatly loves her God

But I call her great because she has a great heart
I call her great because she loves to cook for her family
I call her great because she gardens with a loving hand
I call her great because she greets all with a great smile

Greatly is she loved and greatly is she cared for by all
Her family adores her as does all the grand and great grand kids
But I think she is great because of her great beauty and gentle smile
And not only that but I love her because of the spirit of God
that guides her

It is great to see her pray for her children for their health and success
It is great to find her falling asleep in her great chair,
while reading about God
It is great to see the children run to greet and hug her with
unshakable love
Now you see why a grandmother is a greatly to be loved

Terrence Morrissey

This Heart*

This heart isn't the heart of a staunch true man
This heart is hardened and cold
This heart that once knew love and built my family a house
This heart is now upstretched towards my Lord

This heart once held the heart of a loved one
Entwined with hers, this heart never stood alone
This heart realized its calling with gentleness and love
For this heart was meant to never be forlorn and solitary

Please don't judge me by the pain on my face or what you think I
should be
For this heart has known many failures and been broken
more than once
Some hearts have never been broken but still they know pain
In times past this heart of mine brought me joy and
put a smile on my face

Now this heart is tired and getting old and knows
the pain of loneliness
Life never did turn out just as I planned, you can tell by the
agony in my eyes
This heart cries out to my Lord who sits above
Look at the pain that I suffer and to forgive me for the pain that
I caused others

*An adaptation.

Terrence Morrissey

Today I Really Fell In Love With You

It took me completely by surprise but there was nothing I could do
When I looked into your beautiful brown eyes and
kissed your sweet lips
My beating heart was stilled and my empty arms fulfilled
Because today I really fell in love with you

I hope that you will always be my one true love
It is my prayer that you too will always feel this way
The moment you took my hand in yours and pressed your lips to mine
I looked to heaven with solemn thanks because today I really fell in
love with you

My lonely heart needed you and now my empty arms
are empty no more
My love for you is pure and in your loveliness I truly do delight
I've fallen so deeply in love with you and you have made
my future bright
So let me say it just one more time, today I really fell in love with you'.

Terrence Morrissey

True Love

A whisper of a breeze touched the curl on her forehead
She smiled as though she held the happiness of the world in her heart
A sparkle like the sun bouncing off a diamond danced in her eyes
A spirit of love and peace encompassed the sweetness of her face

She held a single rose as a dew drop from off the petals fell
to the ground
The sound of a love song filled the air as the words touched
her very being
Words of love, happiness and joy entered upon her very soul
Alas, she spoke to the wind and the sun; this is my destiny to behold

Slowly walking across a carpet of grass she melted into his
outstretched arms
He was Irish with that wondrous Irish smile and he held her
hand in his
Holding her close to his breast, his arms gathered round bout her
Slowly ever slowly drawing her closer they embraced
as lover always do

She rested her head upon his shoulder as he kissed that curl
upon her head
They spoke of love and of ecstasies yet to come,
as his lips touched hers
The single rose she held close to her breast burst open
with petals anew
They walked into a golden sunrise and she once more knew true love

Terrence Morrissey

(Untitled)

As 1 look at the faces of the men in this room,
I see shame, regret, defeat and gloom
But there's also a sparkle if I look close into their eyes
A twinkle of hope, if only they'd try.

Someone has been waiting for you all to show,
How you burned your last bridge and had nowhere to go.
He's waiting patiently, knowing one day you would come,
He sits quietly in the back row not caring where from.

Then came the day when you walked through the door,
He smiled inside knowing you would suffer no more.
He walks by your side all through the day,
Through all of your classes, workshops and play.

He listens quietly to your stories of hardship and strain,
Longing to reach out to put an end to your pain.
But instead lie just waits, knowing you wouldn't understand,
That this is all part of His Father's master plan.

He sits by your bedside while you toss and you turn,
Cursing in your sleep of the lessons you've learned.
When you awake in the morning, He's been there all night,
He stayed by your side ready to fight, and he would fight for your soul.

If and when the demons came, he would stand by your side,
And He would fight in God's name.
Now you're feeling much better, you're on day twenty four,
But you felt something pulling as you tried for the door.

It was that someone's hand upon your brow,
Asking "My son, please do not go just now."
You must hear the message I've waited so patiently to give,
I've got news from God. He wants you to live."

Michael Morrissey
Inspired by the Holy Spirit 2005

Waiting For A Phone Call

I wondered why the phone didn't ring
And staring at it didn't do a thing
Pacing the floor wasn't much help
Another cup of coffee might do the trick

But no, the more I paced and stared at that thing
The more I was sure that it wouldn't ring
Perhaps a shower with cold running water
Could take my mind of this darn matter

That was yesterday and the day before
I thought as I once again paced the floor
Hello, hello, I said with the phone to my ear
But shucks it was just a phone on the TV that I hear

"I give up;" I said to myself, I put the phone back on the shelf
Oh well, there is always a chance that today she will call
The next day, when I hung up the phone,
I smiled a smile "I really enjoyed that telephone call"

Terrence Morrissey

Waking Up With You On My Mind

I awoke one early morn; the moon was golden in the sky
I watched as stars sparkled and danced amongst the clouds
And a moonbeam cut a golden path across the heavens
I saw you smile as her eyes danced with laughter

The tree tops swayed in that gilded moment
And an early morning bird sang softly to the dawn
A heaven sent sound that made my heart glad
And in that song you once more smiled for me alone

Softly I heard you sigh as you nestled gently in my arms
The softness of your touch was as a gentle breeze
Caressing my very soul as my heart beat with a song of love
I dreamed a dream of love as I awoke with you on my mind

Terrence Morrissey

Welcome Home

Welcome home my beloved
Where have you been?
You've been missing all of my life
As though you never were there

Sine you returned and I'm with you
I seem to stand so much taller
The sun seems to shine a little brighter
And the blue of the sky is just a little bluer

Welcome home my beloved,
Where have you been?
It has been such a long, long time
In the morning a sweet voice spoke, I'm glad I'm home

Terrence Morrissey

When You Walked By

Your shadow fell across a wilted flower
And in an instant a rose appeared
Your shadow met a gloomy day
And turned the gloom to sunshine
Your shadow fell across a rainy day
And a rainbow lit up the sky
Your shadow fell across a saddened face
And behold a smile appeared
Your shadow encountered sadness one day
And joy and happiness was the result
Your shadow has become a part of me
And I want to be that close to you forever

Terrence Morrissey

Who Else

Who gave the birds their songs to sing?
Who wrote the words, who wrote the melody?
Who put the thrill in the trill as the little bird sang?
Who, you might ask with acceptable awe

Who made the grass, you well may ask?
Who designed the individual blade?
Who made the carpet across the meadow?
Who, you might ask with acceptable awe

Who made the flower, who created the million designs?
Who brought those colors together?
Who ever heard of making a blade of grass?
Who, you might ask with acceptable awe

Who put the rainbow in the sky?
Who designed the colors?
Who placed it so the whole world would see?
Who, you might ask with acceptable awe

Who ever heard of giving songs to the birds?
Who ever heard of placing rainbows on high?
Who else I would answer, who but He
The one and only, who else but God

Copyright by:
Terrence Morrissey

You're The Reason

I awoke in the early morning hours feeling kind of blue
I tossed and I turned and couldn't stop thinking of you
I climbed out of bed walking the floor with you on my mind
So now you know, my beloved that I can't sleep at night

How I wished that there was a knock on my door and it was you
But there was no knock on the door how sad as I looked at the moon
Walking the floor and singing a song wishing you were here
Sweetheart, now you know, you're the reason I can't sleep at night

Like bright golden stars in the sky you are so close but oh so far apart
I dream of our first kiss buried deep within this heart of mine,
whence will it come
I walk the floor all alone, singing a song out of tune, and seeing a
vision of your beauty
I wake alone in the darkness and I know that you're the reason I can't
sleep at night

Terrence Morrissey

Your Picture

Your picture sits gently on the bureau at the foot of my bed
I see your smiling face when I lay me down to sleep
Just as a golden moonbeam greets the darkness of the night
And as a ray of golden sunshine greets the start of each new day
I awake and the picture of your sweet smile greets me
And fills my heart with joy

Terrence Morrissey

An Alphabetical List Of Poems As They Appear In The Book

A BEAUTIFUL EXPRESSION OF LOVE
A BILLOWING CLOUD
A BUTTERFLY SAID IT ALL
A CASTLE IN MY HEART
A CITY FULL OF CHURCHES
A FLOWER AND A SONG
A GENTLE KISS
A GLANCE ACROSS THE SEA
A GREEN EYED BEAUTY AND A HORSE CALLED DURANGO
A HEART JUST LIKE GOD
A HEART OF PAIN
A LOVE POEM FOR A PRINCESS
A MEMORY MADE IN HEAVEN
A NEW LIFE THUS BEGUN
A PRETTY GIRL, A CUP OF COFFEE AND A PUPPY
A ROSE WITHOUT A KISS
A SHATTERED DREAM
A SIMPLE THING
A SLEEP OVER ONCE AGAIN
A SONG OF LOVE
A SONGBIRD AND A FADED TEAR DROP

A TEASING KISS
A WEDDING VOW
A WOMAN LIKE YOU
ADORABLE
ADORING YOU
ALL OVER AGAIN
AN AMAZING GAL
AN ANGEL IN MY ARMS
AN IRISHMAN'S DREAM
AN ODE TO AN OLD MAN WITH ABROKEN HEART
AS LONG AS YOU WALK BACK IN
BEAUTIFUL
BEAUTIFUL AND CHARMING IS MY SWEET LOVE
BEAUTY SPLENDOR AND LOVE
CAPTURED
CLIMB HIGHER by Jim McGregor
DANCING IN HEAVEN
DANCING ON MY MIND
DAWN
DEEP IS MY PAIN
DISCO DAVE
DON'T WAIT ANOTHER DAY
EVE AND HER PARTNER
EYES SO BEAUTIFUL
FIVE LITTLE WORDS
FLOWERS GENTLE BENEAT OUR FEET
FOR ALL ETERNITY
FOREVER ALONE I STAND
FOREVER LOVELY
FROM SADNESS TO GLADNESS
FROM WHENCE DID THIS LOVE SPRING
GRAVITY IT NEVER FAILS
HAND IN HAND

HER PRAYER
HIGH IN THE SKY
HOW CAN I SAY I LOVE YOU
I AM COMMITTED
I DREAMED A DREAM OF LOVE
I GUESS
I KNOW GOD CREATED YOU FOR ME
I LOVED YOU ONCE BEFORE - I CAN LOVE YOU ONCE AGAIN
I WILL NEVER NOT LOVE YOU ALL THE DAYS OF MY LIFE
I WILL NEVER SEE
IF I COULD HAVE MY WAY
IN THE GARDEN OF MY HEART
IT HAPPENED ONE DAY
JUST ASK by Jim McGregor
KNOWING TRUE LOVE ONCE MORE
LAUGHTER AND A SMILE
LIFE OR DEATH – THE CHOICE
LIVING IN A DREAM
LOST IN THE BEAUTY OF YOUR SMILE
LOVE AT LAST ENTWINED
LOVE CAME AND BROKE MY HEART
LOVE ON THE WINGS OF A DOVE
LOVE OVER THE TELEPHONE
MEMORIES AT TWILIGHT
MILES BETWEEN US
MY BELOVED MY PIANO AND ME
MY CHAIR by Jim McGregor
MY HEART WAS ON EVERY RIDE
MY LAST TRUE LOVE
MY LOVE FOR YOU IS….
MY LOVER AND MY FRIEND
MY ONE AND ONLY

THE VOICE OF AN ANGEL
THE WAVE UPON THE SHORE
THEN THERE WERE NONE
THERE IS NO BOND SO SWEET
THERE WAS A MOMENT
THERE'S A FRESHNESS IN THE AIR
THEY CALL HER GREAT GRANDMOTHER
THIS HEART
TODAY I REALLY FELL IN LOVE WITH YOU
TRUE LOVE
UNTITLED by Michael Morrissey
WAITING FOR A PHONE CALL
WAKING UP WITH YOU ON MY MIND
WELCOME HOME
WHEN YOU WALKED BY
WHO ELSE
YOU'E THE REASON
YOUR PICTURE

82722055R00100

Made in the USA
Columbia, SC
20 December 2017